Pat,

Happy New Year! May you grow
deeper in Christ this year. Thanks
for all you do!

Your Brother,

Jeremy

PIERCED
BY THE
WORD

PIERCED
BY THE
WORD

THIRTY – ONE
MEDITATIONS *for your* SOUL

JOHN
PIPER

Multnomah® Publishers *Sisters, Oregon*

PIERCED BY THE WORD
published by Multnomah Publishers, Inc.

© 2003 by Desiring God Foundation
International Standard Book Number: 1-59052-173-0

Cover image by Photonica/Kamil Vojnar

Unless otherwise indicated, Scripture quotations are from:
The Holy Bible, English Standard Version
© 2001 by Crossway Bibles, a division of Good News Publishers.
Used by permission. All rights reserved.
Other Scripture quotations are from:
New American Standard Bible (NASB) © 1960, 1977 by the Lockman Foundation
Revised Standard Version Bible (RSV) © 1946, 1952 by the Division of Christian
Education of the National Council of the Churches of Christ
in the United States of America
Italics in Scripture quotations indicate emphasis added.

Multnomah is a trademark of Multnomah Publishers, Inc.,
and is registered in the U.S. Patent and Trademark Office.
The colophon is a trademark of Multnomah Publishers, Inc.

Printed in the United States of America

For information:
MULTNOMAH PUBLISHERS, INC. • P.O. BOX 1720 • SISTERS, OR 97759

Library of Congress Cataloging-in-Publication Data

Piper, John, 1946-
    Pierced by the word / by John Piper.
        p. cm.
    Includes bibliographical references and index.
    ISBN 1-59052-173-0
    1. Devotional calendars. I. Title.
BV4811 .P56 2003
242'.2--dc21

                                                2003010661

03 04 05 06 07 08—9 8 7 6 5 4 3 2 1 0

BOOKS BY JOHN PIPER

GOD'S PASSION FOR HIS GLORY
Living the Vision of Jonathan Edwards

THE PLEASURES OF GOD
*Meditations on God's Delight
in Being God*

DESIRING GOD
Meditations of a Christian Hedonist

THE DANGEROUS DUTY OF DELIGHT
The Glorified God and the Satisfied Soul

THE PURIFYING POWER
OF LIVING BY FAITH
in FUTURE GRACE

A HUNGER FOR GOD
Desiring God Through Prayer and Fasting

Let the Nations Be Glad!
The Supremacy of God in Missions

A GODWARD LIFE
*Savoring the Supremacy of God
in All of Life*

A GODWARD LIFE, Book Two
*Savoring the Supremacy of God
in All of Life*

SEEING AND SAVORING JESUS CHRIST

THE LEGACY OF SOVEREIGN JOY
*God's Triumphant Grace in the Lives of
Augustine, Luther, and Calvin*

THE HIDDEN SMILE OF GOD
*The Fruit of Affliction in the Lives of
John Bunyan, William Cowper,
and David Brainerd*

THE ROOTS OF ENDURANCE
*Invincible Perseverance in the Lives of
John Newton, Charles Simeon,
and William Wilberforce*

THE MISERY OF JOB AND
THE MERCY OF GOD
(with photography by Ric Ergenbright)

THE INNKEEPER

RECOVERING BIBLICAL MANHOOD AND
WOMANHOOD
A Response to Evangelical Feminism
(edited with Wayne Grudem)

WHAT'S THE DIFFERENCE?
*Manhood and Womanhood
Defined According to the Bible*

THE JUSTIFICATION OF GOD
*An Exegetical and Theological Study
of Romans 9:1–23*

COUNTED RIGHTEOUS IN CHRIST
*Should We Abandon the
Imputation of Christ?*

BROTHERS, WE ARE NOT PROFESSIONALS
A Plea for Radical Ministry

THE SUPREMACY OF GOD
IN PREACHING

BEYOND THE BOUNDS
*Open Theism and the Undermining
of Biblical Christianity*
(edited with Justin Taylor and Paul Kjoss Helseth)

DON'T WASTE YOUR LIFE

*To pastors
who pierce the soul with truth
like surgeons not slayers.*

For the word of God is living and active,
sharper than any two-edged sword,
piercing to the division of soul and of spirit,
of joints and of marrow,
and discerning the thoughts and intentions of the heart.

HEBREWS 4:12

CONTENTS

A WORD TO
THE READER

I LOVE THE WORD OF GOD. I DON'T SAY IT LIGHTLY. It is a terrible thing. "The voice of the LORD…strips the forest bare!" (Psalm 29:9). By His Word, God created the universe. And when His Son comes again, His Word will be like a "sharp sword with which to strike down the nations" (Revelation 19:15). So I tremble before the Word of God.

But this trembling is sweet. There is a promise attached to it. God says, "This is the one to whom I will look: he who is humble and contrite in spirit and *trembles* at my word" (Isaiah 66:2). Not every "look" of God is to be desired. But this one is. It is the look of blessing. And when God blesses the broken and contrite, His Word becomes Life. "Lord, to whom shall we go? You have the words of eternal life" (John 6:68).

Yes, the Word pierces. And there is pain. But for those who trust in the living Word, Jesus Christ, all the piercing will be pleasant in the end. The boil will be lanced. The cancer cut out. The poison removed. For those who trust the severe mercy of Jesus, all piercing is healing.

I pray that these meditations will reveal and not conceal the Word of God. May they become in your life the living embodiment of that Word and penetrate to the deep places of your soul. God has a good work to do there.

John Piper

o n e

HOW STRANGE AND WONDERFUL IS THE LOVE OF CHRIST!

FOR MANY YEARS I HAVE SOUGHT TO UNDERSTAND HOW the God-centeredness of God relates to His love for sinners like us. Most people do not immediately see God's passion for the glory of God as an act of love. One reason for this is that we have absorbed the world's definition of love. It says: You are loved when you are made much of.

The main problem with this definition of love is that when you try to apply it to God's love for us, it distorts reality. God's love for us is *not* mainly His making much of us, but His giving us the ability to enjoy making much of Him forever. In other words, God's love for us keeps God at the center. God's love for us exalts His value and our satisfaction in it. If God's love made us central and focused on our value, it would distract us from what is most precious; namely, Himself. Love labors and suffers to enthrall us with what is infinitely and eternally satisfying: God. Therefore God's love labors and suffers to break our bondage to the idol of self and focus our affections on the treasure of God.

In a surprising way we can see this in the story of Lazarus's sickness and death.

> ¹ Now a certain man was ill, Lazarus of Bethany, the village of Mary and her sister Martha. ² It was Mary who anointed the Lord with ointment and wiped his feet with her hair, whose brother Lazarus was ill. ³ So the sisters sent to him, saying, "Lord, he whom you love is ill." ⁴ But when Jesus heard it he said, "This illness does not lead to death. It is for the glory of God, so that the Son of God may be glorified through it." ⁵ Now Jesus loved Martha and her sister and Lazarus. ⁶ So, when he heard that Lazarus was ill, he stayed two days longer in the place where he was. (John 11:1–6)

Notice three amazing things:

1. Jesus chose to let Lazarus die. Verse 6: "So when he heard that Lazarus was ill, he stayed two days longer in the place where he was." There was no hurry. His intention was not to spare the family grief, but to raise Lazarus from the dead. This is true even if Lazarus was already dead when the messengers reached Jesus. Jesus either let him die or remained longer to make plain that He was in no hurry to immediately relieve the grief. Something more was driving Him.

2. He was motivated by a passion for the glory of God displayed in His own glorious power. In verse 4 He says, "This illness does not lead to death. It is for the glory of God, so that the Son of God may be glorified through it."

3. Nevertheless both the decision to let Lazarus die and the motivation to magnify God were expressions of love for Mary and Martha and Lazarus. John shows this by the way he connected verses 5 and 6: "Now Jesus loved Martha and her sister and Lazarus. *So* [not "yet," which the NIV wrongly inserts]…he stayed two days longer in the place where he was."

Oh, how many people today—even Christians—would murmur at Jesus for callously letting Lazarus die and putting him and Mary and Martha and others through the pain and misery of those days. And if people today saw that this was motivated by Jesus' desire to magnify the glory of God, how many would call this harsh or unloving! What this shows is how far above the glory of God most people value pain-free lives. For most people, love is whatever puts human value and human well-being at the center. So Jesus' behavior is unintelligible to them.

But let us not tell Jesus what love is. Let us not instruct Him how He should love us and make us central. Let us learn from Jesus what love is and what our true well-being is. *Love is doing whatever you need to do to help people see and savor the glory of God in Christ forever and ever.* Love keeps God central. Because the soul was made for God.

Jesus confirms that we are on the right track here by praying for us in John 17:24, "Father, I desire that they also, whom you have given me, may be with me where I am, *to see my glory* that you have given me because you loved me before the foundation of the world." I assume that this prayer is a loving act of Jesus. But what does He ask? He asks that, in the end, we might see His glory. His love for us makes Himself central. Jesus is the one being for whom self-exaltation is the most loving act. This is because the most satisfying reality we could ever know is Jesus. So to give us this reality, He must give us Himself. The love of Jesus drives Him to pray for us, and then die for us, not that *our* value may be central, but that *His glory* may be central, and we may see it and savor it for all eternity. "Father, I desire that they…be with me…*to see my glory*." That is what it means for Jesus to love us. Divine love labors and suffers to enthrall us with what is infinitely and eternally satisfying: God in Christ. That we might see His glory—for that He let Lazarus die, and for that He went to the cross.

O Father, take us captive with this love.
Open the eyes of our hearts to see
and savor the glory of Christ.
And when we are enthralled with
being loved this way, make us lovers like Jesus.
Let us labor and suffer to lead as many
as we can into this all-satisfying love.
In Jesus' name we pray. Amen.

two

GOD *IS* THE GOSPEL

HAVE YOU EVER ASKED WHY GOD'S FORGIVENESS IS OF any value? Or what about eternal life? Have you ever asked why a person would want to have eternal life? Why should we want to live forever? These questions matter because it is possible to want forgiveness and eternal life for reasons that prove you don't have them.

Take forgiveness, for example. You might want God's forgiveness because you are so miserable with guilt feelings. You just want relief. If you can believe that He forgives you, then you will have some relief, but not necessarily salvation. If you only want forgiveness because of emotional relief, you won't have *God's* forgiveness. He does not give it to those who use it only to get His gifts and not Himself.

Or you might want to be healed from a disease or get a good job or find a spouse. Then you hear that God can help you get these things, but that first your sins would have to be forgiven. Someone tells you to believe that Christ died for your sins, and that if you believe this, your sins will be forgiven. So you believe it in order to remove the obstacle to health and job

18 JOHN PIPER

and spouse. Is that gospel salvation? I don't think so.

In other words, it matters what you are hoping for through forgiveness. It matters why you want it. If you want forgiveness only for the sake of savoring the creation, then the Creator is not honored and you are not saved. Forgiveness is precious for one final reason: It enables you to enjoy fellowship with God. If you don't want forgiveness for that reason, you won't have it at all. God will not be used as currency for the purchase of idols.

Similarly, we ask: Why do we want eternal life? One might say: Because hell is the alternative and that's painful. Another might say: Because there will be no sadness there. Another might say: My loved ones have gone there and I want to be with them. Others might dream of endless sex or food. Or more noble fortunes. In all these aims one thing is missing: God.

The saving motive for wanting eternal life is given in John 17:3: "This is eternal life, that they know you the only true God, and Jesus Christ whom you have sent." If we do not want eternal life because it means joy in God, then we won't have eternal life. We simply kid ourselves that we are Christians if we use the glorious gospel of Christ to get what we love more than Christ. The "good news" will not prove good to any for whom God is not the chief good.

Here is the way Jonathan Edwards put it in a sermon to his people in 1731. Read this slowly and let it waken you to the true goodness of forgiveness and life.

> The redeemed have all their objective good in God.
> God Himself is the great good which they are brought
> to the possession and enjoyment of by redemption. He
> is the highest good, and the sum of all that good which

Christ purchased. God is the inheritance of the saints; he is the portion of their souls. God is their wealth and treasure, their food, their life, their dwelling place, their ornament and diadem, and their everlasting honor and glory. They have none in heaven but God; he is the great good which the redeemed are received to at death, and which they are to rise to at the end of the world. The Lord God, he is the light of the heavenly Jerusalem; and is the "river of the water of life" that runs, and the tree of life that grows, "in the midst of the paradise of God." The glorious excellencies and beauty of God will be what will forever entertain the minds of the saints, and the love of God will be their everlasting feast. The redeemed will indeed enjoy other things; they will enjoy the angels, and will enjoy one another: but that which they shall enjoy in the angels, or each other, or in anything else whatsoever, that will yield them delight and happiness, will be what will be seen of God in them.[1]

---

1. Wilson H. Kimnach, Kenneth P. Minkema, and Douglas A. Sweeney, ed., *The Sermons of Jonathan Edwards: A Reader* (New Haven, CT: Yale University Press, 1999), 74–75.

All-satisfying God, forgive us for making
Your good gifts a substitute for You.
We are so prone to mistake the portrait for the person.
Satisfy us with Yourself.
You have promised in the New Covenant,
"They shall all know me from the least to the greatest."
Let this be our portion now—a kind of knowing,
O God, that treasures the One we know.
Let us experience the gospel in its fullness,
which is Christ crucified and risen
for sinners to bring us home to You.
In His name we pray. Amen.

three

PIERCED BY THE WORD OF GOD

A Meditation on Hebrews 4:12

For the word of God is living and active and
sharper than any two-edged sword,
and piercing as far as the division of soul and spirit,
of both joints and marrow, and able to
judge the thoughts and intentions of the heart.

NASB

OH, HOW WE NEED TO KNOW OURSELVES. ARE WE SAVED? Are we alive in Christ? There is only one instrument that creates, detects, and confirms eternal life in the soul of man; namely, the Word of God. What Hebrews 4:12 says about this Word is, therefore, all important. Consider it with me phrase by phrase.

"The word of God"
The term "word of God" may mean a word spoken by God without a human mouthpiece. But in the New Testament it regularly means a word or a message that a human speaks on

God's behalf. So, for example, Hebrews 13:7 says, "Remember your leaders, those who spoke to you the word of God. Consider the outcome of their way of life, and imitate their faith." So the "word of God" in Hebrews 4:12 probably refers to the truth of God revealed in Scripture that humans speak to each other with reliance on God's help to understand it and apply it.

"Living and active"

The Word of God is not a dead word or an ineffective word. It has life in it. And because it has life in it, it produces effects. There is something about the Truth, as God has revealed it, that connects it to God as a source of all life and power. God loves His Word. He is partial to His Word. He honors His Word with His presence and power. If we want our teaching or witness to have power and produce effects, let us stay close to the revealed Word of God.

"Sharper than any two-edged sword, and piercing as far as the division of soul and spirit, of both joints and marrow"

What does this living and effective Word do? It pierces. For what purpose? To divide. To divide what? Soul and spirit. What does that mean?

The writer gives an analogy: It's like dividing joints and marrow. Joints are the thick, hard outer part of the bone. Marrow is the soft, tender, living inner part of the bone. That is an analogy of "soul and spirit." The Word of God is like a sword that is sharp enough to cut right through the outer, hard, tough part of a bone to the inner, soft living part of the bone. Some

swords, less sharp, may strike a bone and glance off and not penetrate. Some swords may penetrate partway through the tough,
thick joint of a bone. But a very sharp, powerful double-edged
sword (sharp on each side of the point) will penetrate the joint
all the way to the marrow. "Soul and spirit" are like "bone joint
and bone marrow." "Soul" is that invisible dimension of our life
that we are by nature. "Spirit" is what we are by supernatural
rebirth. Jesus said, "That which is born of the flesh is flesh, and
that which is born of the Spirit is spirit" (John 3:6). Without the
awakening, creative, regenerating work of the Spirit of God in
us we are merely "natural" rather than "spiritual" (1 Corinthians
2:14–15). So the "spirit" is that invisible dimension of our life
that we are by the regenerating work of the Spirit.

What then is the point in saying that the "word of God"
pierces to the "division of soul and spirit"? The point is that it's
the Word of God that reveals to us our true selves. Are we spiritual or are we natural? Are we born of God and spiritually alive,
or are we deceiving ourselves and spiritually dead? Are the
"thoughts and intentions of our hearts" spiritual thoughts and
intentions or only natural thoughts and intentions? Only the
"word of God" can "judge the thoughts and intentions of the
heart" as Hebrews 4:12 says.

Practically speaking, when we read or hear "the word of
God" we sense ourselves pierced. The effect of this piercing is to
reveal whether there is spirit or not. Is there marrow and life in
our bones? Or are we only a "skeleton" with no living marrow?
Is there "spirit," or only "soul"? The Word of God pierces deep
enough to show us the truth of our thoughts and our motives
and our selves.

Give yourselves to this Word of God, the Bible. Use it to know yourself and confirm your own spiritual life. If there is life, there will be love and joy and a heart to obey the Word. Give yourself to this Word so that your words become the Word of God for others and reveal to them their own spiritual condition. Then in the wound of the Word, pour the balm of the Word.

Oh, how we love Your Word, Father!
It is precious beyond all earthly treasures.
Incline our hearts to this Word,
and break our bondage to other things.
Let us see wonders in it.
Pierce through our soul and waken spiritual life.
Confirm the marrow of our faith and make us real,
through and through. Forbid that we would be false to Your
faithfulness, and make us mighty in the Spirit.
Through Christ, we pray. Amen.

four

BE NOT MERE
SHADOWS AND ECHOES

WE ARE NOT GOD. SO BY COMPARISON TO ULTIMATE, absolute Reality, we are not much. Our existence is secondary and dependent on the absolute Reality of God. He is the only Given in the universe. We are derivative. He always was and had no beginning. So He was not given form by another. We were. He simply is. But we become. "I Am Who I Am" is His name (Exodus 3:14).

Nevertheless, because He made us with the highest creaturely purpose in mind—to enjoy and display the Creator's glory—we may have a very substantial life that lasts forever. This is why we were made ("All things were created through Him and *for Him*," Colossians 1:16). This is why our sexuality was redeemed ("Flee from sexual immorality.... You are not your own, for you were bought with a price. So *glorify God in your body*," 1 Corinthians 6:18, 20). This is why we eat and drink ("So, whether you eat or drink, or whatever you do, *do all to the glory of God*," 1 Corinthians 10:31). This is why we pray ("Whatever you ask the Father in my name, this I will do, *that the Father may be glorified in the Son*," John 14:13). This is why we do all good deeds ("Let your light shine before others, so that they may see your good works and *give glory to your Father* who is in heaven," Matthew 5:16).

That is why we exist—to display the glory of God. Human life is all about God. That is the meaning of being human. It is our created nature to make much of God. It is our glory to worship the glory of God. When we fulfill this reason for being, we have substance. There is weight and significance in our existence. Knowing, enjoying, and thus displaying the glory of God is a sharing in the glory of God. Not that we become God. But something of His greatness and beauty is on us as we realize this purpose for our being—to image-forth His excellence. This is our substance.

Not to fulfill this purpose for human existence is to be a mere *shadow* of the substance we were created to have. Not to display God's worth by enjoying Him above all things is to be a mere *echo* of the music we were created to make.

This is a great tragedy. Humans are not made to be mere shadows and echoes. We were made to have God-like substance and make God-like music and have God-like impact. That is what it means to be created in the image of God (Genesis 1:27). But when humans forsake their Maker and love other things more, they become like the things they love—small, insignificant, weightless, inconsequential, and God-diminishing.

Listen to the way the psalmist puts it: "The idols of the nations are silver and gold, the work of human hands. They have mouths, but they do not speak; they have eyes, but they do not see; they have ears, but they do not hear, nor is there any breath in their mouths. *Those who make them become like them, so do all who trust in them*" (Psalm 135:15–18; see also 115:4–8).

Think and tremble. You become like the man-made things that you trust: mute, blind, deaf. This is a shadow existence. It is an echo of what you were meant to be. It is an empty mime on the stage of history with much movement and no meaning.

Dear reader, be not shadows and echoes. Break free from the epidemic of the manward spirit of our age. Set your face like flint to see and know and enjoy and live in the light of the Lord. "O house of Jacob, come, let us walk in the light of the LORD" (Isaiah 2:5). In His light you will see *Him* and all things as they truly are. You will wake up from the slumbers of shadowland existence. You will crave and find substance. You will make God-like music with your life. Death will but dispatch you to paradise. And what you leave behind will not be a mere shadow or echo, but a tribute on earth, written in heaven, to the triumphant grace of God.

∞

O Father, how we fear the wasting of our years!
Forgive us for our love affair with empty things and our little
love for You. Make us feel the suicidal faith in innocent idols.
Give us fresh freedom from all hollow gems.
Grant us to bear the weight of glory and become more like Your
Son. In His all-sustaining name we pray. Amen.

HOW TO DRINK ORANGE JUICE TO THE GLORY OF GOD

WHEN I AM ASKED, "IS THE DOCTRINE OF TOTAL Depravity biblical?" my answer is, "Yes." One thing I mean by this is that all of our actions (apart from saving grace) are morally ruined. In other words, everything an unbeliever does is sinful and thus unacceptable to God.

One of my reasons for believing this comes from 1 Corinthians 10:31. "So, whether you eat or drink, or whatever you do, do all to the glory of God." Is it sin to disobey this biblical commandment? Yes.

So I draw this somber conclusion: It is sin to eat or drink or do anything *not* for the glory of God. In other words, sin is not just a list of harmful things (killing, stealing, etc.). Sin is leaving God out of account in the ordinary affairs of your life. Sin is anything you do that you don't do for the glory of God.

But what do unbelievers do for the glory of God? Nothing. Therefore everything they do is sinful. That is what I mean by saying that, apart from saving grace, all we do is morally ruined.

This, of course, raises the practical question: Well, how *do* you "eat and drink" to the glory of God? Say, orange juice for breakfast?

One answer is found in 1 Timothy 4:3–5:

> [Some] forbid marriage and require abstinence from foods that God created to be received with thanksgiving by those who believe and know the truth. For everything created by God is good, and nothing is to be rejected if it is received with thanksgiving, for it is made holy by the word of God and prayer.

Orange juice was "created to be received with *thanksgiving* by those who *believe*…the truth." Therefore, *un*believers cannot use orange juice for the purpose God intended—namely, as an occasion for heartfelt *thanksgiving* to God from a true heart of *faith*.

But believers can, and this is how they glorify God. Their drinking orange juice is "made holy by the word of God and prayer" (1 Timothy 4:5). The *Word of God* teaches us that juice, and even our strength to drink it, is a free gift of God (1 Corinthians 4:7; 1 Peter 4:11). The *prayer* is our humble response of thanks from the heart. *Believing* this truth in the Word and offering *thanks* in prayer is one way we drink orange juice to the glory of God.

The other way is to drink lovingly. For example, don't insist on the biggest helping. This is taught in the context of 1 Corinthians 10:33, "I try to please everyone in everything I do, *not seeking my own advantage, but that of many, that they may be saved.*" "Be imitators of me, as I am of Christ" (1 Corinthians 11:1). Everything we do—even drinking orange juice—can be done with the intention and hope that it will be to the advantage of many that they may be saved.

Let us praise God that we have escaped by His grace from the total ruin of all our deeds. And let us do everything, whether we eat or drink, to the glory of our great God!

❧

Father, every good gift is from You.
Even the ability to receive them is from You.
We love to declare our dependence on
You for the smallest and the greatest things.
Grant that nothing in our lives
will be disconnected from You.
Make us conscious all the time that
everything gets its proper meaning
from how it relates to You.
May it be our joy to join our orange juice—
and everything else—to Your grace.
With overflowing thanks, we pray, in Jesus' name. Amen.

six

BIG, SWEEPING—
BUT NOT INSIPID—
PRAYERS

One of the amazing things about the prayers of the Bible is how big and sweeping they often are. Yet they don't have the vague ring of "God bless the missionaries" that sounds so weak. We sometimes try to remedy this by saying, "We should pray specific prayers for specific people and specific needs, and not vague general prayers." There is truth to that. We should pray that way.

But there is another reason why our big general prayers seem insipid, while the big Bible prayers don't. Ours often don't have much of God in them, and don't articulate what the great spiritual things are that we want God to do for "the missionaries" or "the nations" or "the world" or "the lost." The words "God bless" would not sound so weak and vague if we said what the blessing would look like. There is a world of difference between "Lord, help our missionaries" and "Lord, help our missionaries to drink deep at the river of Your delights." Or, "Lord, help our missionaries rejoice in tribulations and remember that tribulation works endurance and endurance hope."

Big general prayers become powerful when they are filled up with concrete, radical biblical goals for the people we are praying for. "Hallowed be thy name...thy will be done on earth as in heaven," is a huge, sweeping prayer. But it asks for two concrete things: that in all the world God's name would be regarded as precious, and that hearts would be changed to do God's will with the same zeal and purity that the angels have in heaven.

It is mentioning these spiritual goals with passion that turns insipid generalizations into dynamite generalizations. So don't shrink back from praying huge, sweeping prayers. For example, in Ephesians 6:18 Paul says that we should be "praying at all times in the Spirit, with all prayer and supplication...for all the saints." Think of it! What an incredible breadth and generality. ALL the saints! Do you do that? Pray for *all* the saints? I admit I do not do it often enough. My heart is too small. But I am trying to get my heart around it. The Bible commands it.

This will not sound silly, like "God bless all the saints." It will sound robust and cataclysmic, like, "God, look upon your entire church everywhere and have mercy to waken her and give her new life and hope and doctrinal purity and holiness so that all the saints stand strong for your glory in the day of temptation and distress."

Let's pray some huge prayers for billions of lost people and thousands of peoples in the "10/40 Window." Paul said, "Finally, brothers, pray for us, that the word of the Lord may speed ahead and be honored, as happened among you" (2 Thessalonians 3:1). Oh, that God would do that speeding work in our day! I encourage all of my readers to go out and buy

Patrick Johnstone's *Operation World*—a truth-laden prayer guide for all the countries of the world. Then pray some huge, sweeping prayers for the peoples and the missionaries of this vast region called the 10/40 Window.

The 10/40 Window extends from West Africa to East Asia, and from ten degrees north to forty degrees south of the equator. This specific region contains three of the world's dominant religious blocs. The majority of those darkened in unbelief by Islam, Hinduism, and Buddhism live within the 10/40 Window. It is home to the majority of the world's unevangelized people.

While it constitutes only one-third of earth's total land area, the 10/40 Window is home to nearly two-thirds of the world's people, with a total population nearing four billion. Of the world's 50 least evangelized countries, 37 are within the 10/40 Window. Yet those 37 countries comprise 95 percent of the total population of the 50 least evangelized countries!

Of the poorest of the poor, more than eight out of ten live in the 10/40 Window. On average, they exist on less than $500 per person per year. Although 2.4 billion of these people live within the 10/40 Window, only 8 percent of all missionaries work among them. Surely this is worth some big, sweeping, biblical prayers!

Great God of overflowing grace,
move our hearts to pray for
Your saving power among the nations.
Burden us with the plight of peoples who
have no access to the gospel.
Grant us to pray big, global,
God-sized, Bible-saturated prayers.
Don't let us lose sight of the one lost sheep nearby.
But, O Father, give us a passion for Your
worldwide purpose to call Your sheep from
every people on the earth.
For the glory of Christ,
and in His name we pray. Amen.

seven

WHAT IS HUMILITY?

IN 1908 THE BRITISH WRITER G. K. CHESTERTON described the embryo of today's full-grown, adolescent culture called postmodernism. It's already a worn-out phrase. Someday readers will have to look it up in a history book. One mark of its "vulgar relativism" (as Michael Novak calls it)[1] is the hijacking of the word *arrogance* to refer to conviction and *humility* to refer to doubt. Chesterton saw it coming:

> What we suffer from today is humility in the wrong place. Modesty has moved from the organ of ambition. Modesty has settled upon the organ of conviction; where it was never meant to be. A man was meant to be doubtful about himself, but undoubting about the truth; this has been exactly reversed. Nowadays the part of a man that a man does assert is exactly the part he ought not to assert—himself. The part he doubts is exactly the part he ought not to doubt—the Divine Reason.… The new skeptic is so humble that he doubts

---

1. Michael Novak, "Awakening from Nihilism," *First Things,* no. 45 (August/September, 1994), 20–21 (available at www.firstthings.com/ftissues/ft9408/articles/novak.html).

if he can even learn…. There is a real humility typical of our time; but it so happens that it's practically a more poisonous humility than the wildest prostrations of the ascetic…. The old humility made a man doubtful about his efforts, which might make him work harder. But the new humility makes a man doubtful about his aims, which make him stop working altogether…. We are on the road to producing a race of man too mentally modest to believe in the multiplication table.[2]

We have seen it, for example, in the resentment over Christians expressing the conviction that Jewish people (like everyone else) need to believe on Jesus to be saved. The most common response to this conviction is that Christians are arrogant. Modern-day humility is firmly rooted in the relativism that recoils from knowing truth and naming error. But that is not what humility used to mean.

Well, if humility is not compliance with the popular demands of relativism, what is it? This is important, since the Bible says, "God opposes the proud but gives grace to the humble" (1 Peter 5:5), and "Everyone who exalts himself will be humbled, and he who humbles himself will be exalted" (Luke 14:11). So humility is tremendously important. God has told us at least five things about humility.

1. Humility begins with a sense of subordination to God in Christ. "A disciple is not above his teacher, nor a servant above his master" (Matthew 10:24). "Humble yourselves, therefore, under the mighty hand of God" (1 Peter 5:6).

---

2. G. K. Chesteron, *Orthodoxy* (Garden City, NY: Doubleday, 1957), 31–32.

2. Humility does not feel it has a right to better treatment than Jesus got. "If they have called the master of the house Beelzebul, how much more will they malign those of his household" (Matthew 10:25). Therefore humility does not return evil for evil. It is not a life based on its perceived rights. "Christ also suffered for you, leaving you an example, so that you might follow in his steps.... When he suffered, he did not threaten, but continued entrusting to him who judges justly" (1 Peter 2:21–23).

3. Humility asserts truth not to bolster the ego with control or with triumphs in debate, but as service to Christ and love to the adversary. Love "rejoices with the truth" (1 Corinthians 13:6). "What I [Jesus] tell you in the dark, say in the light.... Do not fear" (Matthew 10:27–28). "What we proclaim is not ourselves, but Jesus Christ as Lord, with ourselves as your servants for Jesus' sake" (2 Corinthians 4:5).

4. Humility knows it is dependent on grace for all knowing and believing. "What do you have that you did not receive? If then you received it, why do you boast as if you did not receive it?" (1 Corinthians 4:7). "In humility receive the word implanted, which is able to save your souls" (James 1:21, NASB).

5. Humility knows it is fallible, and so considers criticism and learns from it; but also knows that God has made provision for human conviction and that He calls us to persuade others.

"Now we see in a mirror dimly, but then face to face. Now I know in part; then I shall know fully, even as I have been fully known" (1 Corinthians 13:12). "A wise man listens to advice" (Proverbs 12:15). "Therefore, knowing the fear of the Lord, we persuade others" (2 Corinthians 5:11).

O Father, as much as it lies within us,
we humble ourselves under Your mighty hand.
Have mercy on us in our battle with pride,
and help us put to death all that is
arrogant and self-exalting in our lives.
Show us our utter helplessness without You,
and the sweetness of Your undeserved mercy.
Grant us to walk in meekness and lowliness of spirit,
and to make known the greatness of Christ.
In His name we pray. Amen.

eight

WILDERNESS, WORSHIP, TREASON, AND GOD

A Meditation on Psalm 63

A PSALM OF DAVID,
WHEN HE WAS IN THE WILDERNESS OF JUDAH.

O God, you are my God; earnestly I seek you; my soul thirsts for you; my flesh faints for you, as in a dry and weary land where there is no water. ² So I have looked upon you in the sanctuary, beholding your power and glory. ³ Because your steadfast love is better than life, my lips will praise you. ⁴ So I will bless you as long as I live; in your name I will lift up my hands. ⁵ My soul will be satisfied as with fat and rich food, and my mouth will praise you with joyful lips, ⁶ when I remember you upon my bed, and meditate on you in the watches of the night; ⁷ for you have been my help, and in the shadow of your wings I will sing for joy. ⁸ My soul clings to you; your right hand upholds me. ⁹ But those who seek to destroy my life shall go down into the depths of the earth; ¹⁰ they shall be given over to the power of the sword; they shall be a portion for jackals. ¹¹ But the king shall rejoice in God; all who swear by him shall exult, for the mouths of liars will be stopped.

THE WRITER IS DAVID WHEN HE WAS KING (VERSES 1, 11). The situation is that someone was seeking to destroy his life (verse 9). This corresponds to the time when Absalom, his own son, drove him out of Jerusalem (2 Samuel 15:23). Put yourself in David's place. His son is not just alienated, but hostile enough to want to see his father killed. Here is mortal danger mixed with heartbreaking estrangement from his son.

Learn from David what to do in this brokenhearted, terrifying moment. He prays. The whole psalm is addressed to God. He asks for one thing—not protection, not victory, but God Himself, satisfying his soul, like water satisfies thirst in a dry and weary land. "O God, you are my God; earnestly I seek you; my flesh faints for you, as in a dry and weary land where there is no water" (verse 1). There are seasons of pain and loss and grief and darkness when nothing is worth asking for but God. Everything else seems trivial, even life.

That's why David said in verse 3, "Because your steadfast love is better than life, my lips will praise you." David may well be killed during the night by some plotting traitor sold out to Absalom. How do you sleep? You remind yourself that the love of God in the presence of God is better than not being stabbed to death in the night. But this rest in God's steadfast love is not easily felt. We say the words. But do we feel the reality? David did not feel it as he wanted to feel it. That is why he cried out, "Earnestly I seek you; my soul thirsts for you." David desperately needed God to answer his cry to come and help him taste—not just know, but feel—that God's steadfast love is better than life.

Oh, to know God like this! Would this not be everything

to us? Would this not be more than all riches and fame and success and health, indeed all the world can offer? God Himself coming near and making our souls drink from His love until all else fades from view, and fear is swallowed up in the unshakable security of everlasting enjoyment at the right hand of God. Oh, that we would come to this place in our walk with God! When the saving of David's own life and the rescue of his own son cease to be his gods, and God alone engulfs him in the solid joy of unshakable love, then he will sing for joy in the sorrows of this night, and even perhaps, if God wills, win back his son.

How did God come to David and awaken his spiritual taste, so that he could see God and "be satisfied as with fat and rich food" (verse 5)? The answer is that David remembered the days of worship in the house of God: "So I have looked upon you in the sanctuary, beholding your power and glory" (verse 2). David had been driven from Jerusalem, the place of corporate worship with God's people. And in his distress, he remembers what it was like, and what he saw of God in worship.

Here is a great longing I have for the corporate worship in our churches—that when we meet and sing and pray and hear the Word of God, God Himself will be so manifestly present in "power and glory" that in the years to come, when any of you is cut off from this immeasurable privilege, the very memory of seeing God in worship will bring Him home to you again.

Would you pray with me that God will meet us like that? Would you pray for your pastors and other worship leaders that God would give them songs and prayers and silence and Scriptures and sermons that are so full of the truth of God and the Spirit of God that we will all taste and see that the steadfast love of God is better than life—and all that life can give?

And would you pray for yourselves and for all the people that Saturday nights and Sunday mornings would become seasons of preparation for meeting God—vestibules of the holy place of worship? Pray with David, "O God, you are my God; earnestly I seek you; my soul thirsts for you, my flesh faints for you, as in a dry and weary land where there is no water." If this were on our lips Saturday night and Sunday morning, would not God open the springs of heaven and show us mightily that His "steadfast love is better than life"?

And so, Father, this is the cry of our hearts:
to taste and see that You are good.
Cut away the calluses of our spiritual tongues
and give us taste buds that savor the
reality of Christ in His Word.
Forbid that the rebellion of our
children would weaken our faith.
May the heartaches and the dangers
of life drive us to You, our joy and rest.
In Jesus' name we pray. Amen.

nine

HOW TO BE A REFUGE FOR YOUR CHILDREN

A Meditation on Proverbs 14:26

In the fear of the LORD one has strong confidence,
And his children will have a refuge.

IF DADDY IS AFRAID, WHERE CAN A LITTLE CHILD TURN? Daddies are supposed to be safe. They are supposed to know what to do and how to solve problems and fix things and, most of all, how to protect the children from harm. But what happens if a child sees fear in Daddy's face? What if Daddy is as scared as the child and doesn't know what to do? Then the child is utterly distraught and feels panic. He feels that the one strong and good and reliable place of safety is no longer safe.

But if Daddy is confident, then the children have a refuge. If Daddy is not panicking, but calm and steady, all the walls can come tumbling down, and all the waves can break, and all the snakes hiss and the lions roar and the winds blow, and there will still be a safe place in Daddy's arms. Daddy is a refuge, as long as Daddy is confident. That's why Proverbs 14:26 says that "his children will have a refuge," if Daddy has a "strong confidence." Daddy's confidence is the refuge of his children.

Dads, the battle to be confident is not just about us, it is about the security of our children. It is about their sense of security and happiness. It's about whether they grow up fretful or firm in faith. Until children can know God in a deep, personal way, we are the image and the embodiment of God in their lives. If we are confident and reliable and safe for them, they will much more likely cleave to God as their refuge when the storms break over them later.

So how shall we have "strong confidence"? After all, we, too, are little children; clay pots, weak and broken and battling anxieties and doubts. Is the solution to put on the best show we can and hide our true selves? That will lead to ulcers at best, and God-dishonoring, teenager-repelling duplicity at worst. That is not the answer.

Proverbs 14:26 gives another answer: "In the fear of the LORD there is strong confidence." This is very strange. It says that the solution to fear is fear. The solution to timidity is fear. The solution to uncertainty is fear. The solution to doubt is fear.

How can this be?

Part of the answer is that the "fear of the LORD" means fearing to dishonor the Lord. Which means fearing to distrust the Lord. Which means fearing to fear anything that the Lord has promised to help you overcome. In other words, the fear of the Lord is the great fear destroyer.

If the Lord says, "Fear not, for I am with you; be not dismayed, for I am your God; I will strengthen you, I will help you" (Isaiah 41:10), then it is a fearful thing to worry about the problem He says He will help you with. Fearing that problem when He says, "Fear not, I will help you," is a vote of no confidence against God's Word, and that is a great dishonor to God. And the fear of the Lord trembles to dishonor God like that.

The Lord says, "I will never leave you nor forsake you.' So we can confidently say, 'The Lord is my helper; I will not fear; what can man do to me?'" (Hebrews 13:5–6). If the Lord says that to you, then not to be confident in the Lord's promised presence and help is a kind of pride. It puts our reckoning of the trouble above God's. That is why we read the amazing words of the Lord in Isaiah 51:12, "I, I am he who comforts you; who are you that you are afraid of man who dies, of the son of man who is made like grass?" Who are you to fear man, when God has promised to help you? So it is pride to fear man. And pride is the exact opposite of the fear of God.

So, yes, the Proverb is true and a great help to us. Fear God, dads. Fear God. Fear dishonoring Him. Fear distrusting Him. Fear putting your assessment of the problem above His. He says He can help. He is smarter. He is stronger. He is more generous. Trust Him. Fear not to trust Him.

Why? He works for those who wait for Him (Isaiah 64:4). He will solve the problem. He will rescue the family. He will take care of the little ones. He will meet your needs. Fear distrusting that promise. Then your children will have a refuge. They will have a daddy who "has strong confidence"—not in himself, but in the promises of God, which he trembles not to trust.

Father, we are weak in ourselves.

And our children need us to be strong.

Make us strong in the Lord.

Make Yourself the strength of our lives.

Give us a deep, God-rooted confidence and strength.

Let the children feel it and be secure.

Show them, by our humble faith,

that this safety is in God and not the best of human dads.

So grow them up to be strong in

You from generation to generation.

In Jesus' name we pray. Amen.

GOING DEEP WITH GOD BY HAVING HIM CARRY OUR LOADS

One of the reasons we don't know God deeply is that we don't venture much on His pledge to carry things for us. Knowing God with a sense of authentic personal reality is not merely a matter of study. It is a matter of walking with Him through fire and not being burned. It is a matter of not being crushed under a load because He carries it for you at your side. What, then, does He carry?

1. God Has Carried Our Sins

Isaiah 53:11, "By his knowledge shall the righteous one, my servant, make many to be accounted righteous, and *he shall bear their iniquities.*" Hebrews 9:28, "Christ, having been offered once *to bear the sins of many.*" 1 Peter 2:24, "*He himself bore our sins* in his body on the tree."

Believing this and experiencing its liberating effect is crucial *for life now.* Guilt feelings do not have the last word! It is also crucial *for the hour of our dying.* The sting of death is sin, but thanks be to God, it was removed. It is crucial, too, *for everlasting joy.*

Christ's sin-bearing work secures for us never-ending compensation for every so-called "loss" in this life of sacrificial love. This confidence is the foundation of knowing God.

2. God Pledges to Carry Our Anxieties

1 Peter 5:7, "[*Cast*] *all your anxiety on him*, because he cares for you." The only other place this word for "cast " occurs is in Luke 19:35, where the disciples threw their coats on the colt for Jesus to ride.

What worries does God aim to take from our backs and carry for us? Every kind. For example, anxieties about lacking necessities (Philippians 4:4–7), uselessness (Isaiah 55:11), weakness (2 Corinthians 12:9), decisions (Psalm 32:8), opponents (Romans 8:31), affliction (Psalm 34:19; Romans 5:3–5), aging (Isaiah 46:4), dying (Romans 14:7–9), and not persevering (Philippians 1:6; Hebrews 7:25).

When George Müller was asked how he could be so calm in the middle of a hectic day with so many uncertainties in the orphanage, he answered something like, "I rolled sixty things onto the Lord this morning." When Hudson Taylor was told about missionaries in his charge being in trouble, he was heard soon after whistling his favorite hymn, "Jesus, I Am Resting, Resting in the Joy of What Thou Art."

3. God Pledges to Carry Our Burdens

Psalm 55:22, "*Cast your burden on the LORD,* and he will sustain you; he will never permit the righteous to be moved." The word for "burden" here is *lot.* What is your lot in life today? What has providence brought you? In the end, this is of the Lord. And He will carry it for you. It is not meant to crush you or carry you away. It is meant to test your trust in God to carry it for you. (See also Psalm 16:5; 63:8.)

For Amy Carmichael the "lot" was singleness. There were several chances to leave it and take "the other life." But she heard the inner voice, *No, no, no.* She handed this over to the Lord and He carried it for her and made her fruitful and full of joy.

4. God Pledges to Carry the Cause of Justice for Us

1 Peter 2:23, "When he was reviled, [Jesus] did not revile in return; when he suffered, he did not threaten, but continued *handing over to him who judges justly*" (author's translation).

In almost every relationship of life you will be treated unjustly. "Jesus never called us to a fair fight" (George Otis, Jr.). How will you not be embittered? By letting God carry your cause and settle accounts either on the cross or in hell. Peter said that Jesus handled the wrongs done to him by "handing over" to God who would judge all things justly. God will manage our cause. "'Vengeance is mine, I will repay' says the Lord" (Romans 12:19). Leave it to Him. Prepare to be treated unjustly, whether it is someone breaking in front of you in line or bearing false witness at the final trial of your life.

5. God Pledges to Carry You—All Your Life

Isaiah 46:3–4, "Hearken to me, O house of Jacob, all the remnant of the house of Israel, who have been borne by me from your birth, carried from the womb; even to your old age I am He, and to gray hairs I will carry you. I have made, and I will bear; I will carry and will save" (RSV). (See also Exodus 19:4; Psalm 18:35; 94:18.)

The Christian life is a life of being carried from beginning to end. We work. Yet it is not we, but God who works within us (1 Corinthians 15:10).

Conclusion

So come to Him, all you who labor and are heavy laden, and find rest for your soul. Go deep with God and know Him better by venturing more on His pledge to carry you and all your concerns.

Father, thank You for the zeal You have to be strong for us.
We love Your passion to show Your greatness
by serving us rather than being served by us.
We love to magnify Your strength by
casting our burdens on You.
O Father, help us to be childlike.
Help us not to resent our need for You.
Help us to trust that Your mighty
power is for us in Christ Jesus.
So make us lionhearted in the cause of love.
Through Christ we pray. Amen.

eleven

PERSEVERE IN PRAYER!

A Meditation on Colossians 4

Continue steadfastly in prayer,
being watchful in it with thanksgiving.
At the same time, pray also for us,
that God may open to us a door for the word,
to declare the mystery of Christ…
that I may make it clear, which is how I ought to speak.
COLOSSIANS 4:2–4

THIS TEXT GIVES FIVE GUIDELINES FOR PRAYER THAT WE need to hear.

First, "Continue steadfastly in prayer." There is so much power to be had in persevering prayer. Don't forget the "importunate friend" of Luke 11:8 ("Because of his persistence he will get up and give him as much as he needs" NASB), and don't forget the parable Jesus told to the effect that we "ought always to pray and not lose heart" (Luke 18:1–8). Perseverance is the great test of genuineness in the Christian life. I praise God for Christians who have persevered in prayer sixty, seventy, or eighty years! Oh, let us be a praying people, and let this year—and all our years—be saturated with prayers to the Lord of all power and all good. It will be good to say in the end, "I have finished the race, I have kept the faith"—through prayer.

Second, "Be watchful in your prayers." This means, Be alert! Be mentally awake! Paul probably learned this from the story of what happened in Gethsemane. Jesus asked the disciples to pray, but found them sleeping. So He said to Peter, "Could you not watch one hour? Watch and pray that you may not enter into temptation" (Mark 14:37–38). We must be on the watch as we pray—on the watch against wandering minds, against vain repetitions, against trite and meaningless expressions, against limited, selfish desires. And we should also watch for what is good. We should especially be alert to God's guidance of our prayers in Scripture. It is God who works in us the will to pray, but we always experience this divine enabling as our own resolve and decision.

Third, be thankful in all your prayers. The stories of what God has done in so many lives through renewed prayer are amazing. They have often stirred me up to press on in prayer with thanksgiving. Keep sharing with others these good things.

Fourth, pray that a door would be opened for the Word in your life. In two senses: 1) that there be open, receptive hearts in your church from week to week; and 2) that your neighbors will be open to the gospel as you share it. "The Lord opened [Lydia's] heart to give heed to what was said by Paul" (Acts 16:14). That is what we should want to happen on Sundays and during the week.

Fifth, pray for the preachers of our land that they may make the mystery of Christ clear. "Great…is the mystery of godliness" (1 Timothy 3:16). And oh, what a calling to proclaim it! I love the preaching office! But it is above me. I, and every preaching pastor, need prayer—that we understand the mystery of Christ, that we choose needed texts, that we preach in the power of the Holy Spirit, that we speak the truth in love. Without Christ we can do nothing.

Merciful Father, thank You for being a prayer-hearing God.
Oh, that we would cherish this gift.
It is an overwhelming thought that the
Creator and sustainer of all things gives
heed to our prayers and meets our needs.
Make us persistent and watchful and
thankful and ready for every open door.
Fill our mouths with prayer to You and gospel to others.
Increase our faith in the truth that by prayer
we have an influence in the world all out of
proportion with how small we are.
In Jesus' name we pray. Amen.

DOROTHY SAYERS ON WHY HELL IS A NONNEGOTIABLE

TODAY BELONGS TO THE SOUND BITE; TOMORROW belongs to marketing; eternity belongs to the Truth. If you live only for this world, you will care little for truth. "Let us eat and drink, for tomorrow we die." And if that's all there is, we may as well call the ideas that protect our appetites "truths." But if you live for eternity, you will forego a few fads in order to be everlastingly relevant.

We need to prize truth above temporary successes. Where truth is minimized and people are not rooted and grounded in it, successes are superficial and the growing tree is hollow even while it blooms in the sunshine of prosperity. May God give us a humble, submissive love for the truth of God's Word in the depth and fullness of it.

Listen to Paul's warning about our day: "The time is coming when people will not endure sound teaching; but having itching ears they will accumulate for themselves teachers to suit their own passions (2 Timothy 4:3). "[They] are perishing, because *they refused to love the truth* and so be saved" (2 Thessalonians 2:10).

pierced by the word 55

Take one truth that is not popular and is being abandoned by many who fly the banner of "evangelical" over their tent—the truth of hell. Oh, what a difference it makes when one believes in hell—with trembling and with tears. There is a seriousness over all of life, and an urgency in all our endeavors, and a flavor of blood-earnestness that seasons everything and makes sin feel more sinful, and righteousness feel more righteous, and life feel more precious, and relationships feel more profound, and God appear more weighty.

Nevertheless, as in every generation, there are fresh abandonments of the truth. Clark Pinnock, a Canadian theologian who still calls himself an evangelical, wrote:

> I was led to question the traditional belief in everlasting conscious torment because of moral revulsion and broader theological considerations, not first of all on scriptural grounds. It just does not make any sense to say that a God of love will torture people forever for sins done in the context of a finite life…. It's time for evangelicals to come out and say that the biblical and morally appropriate doctrine of hell is annihilation, not everlasting torment."[1]

Dorothy Sayers, who died in 1957, speaks a necessary antidote to this kind of abandonment of truth.

> There seems to be a kind of conspiracy, especially among middle-aged writers of vaguely liberal tendency,

---

1. Clark Pinnock and Delwin Brown, *Theological Crossfire: An Evangelical/Liberal Dialogue* (Grand Rapids, MI: Zondervan, 1990), 226–27.

to forget, or to conceal, where the doctrine of Hell comes from. One finds frequent references to the "cruel and abominable mediaeval doctrine of hell," or "the childish and grotesque mediaeval imagery of physical fire and worms."...

> But the case is quite otherwise; let us face the facts. The doctrine of hell is not "mediaeval": it is Christ's. It is not a device of "mediaeval priestcraft" for frightening people into giving money to the church: it is Christ's deliberate judgment on sin. The imagery of the undying worm and the unquenchable fire derives, not from "mediaeval superstition," but originally from the Prophet Isaiah, and it was Christ who emphatically used it.... It confronts us in the oldest and least "edited" of the gospels: it is explicit in many of the most familiar parables and implicit in many more: it bulks far larger in the teaching than one realizes, until one reads the Evangelists through instead of picking out the most comfortable texts: one cannot get rid of it without tearing the New Testament to tatters. We cannot repudiate Hell without altogether repudiating Christ.[2]

I would only add: There are many other things which, if abandoned, will also mean the eventual repudiation of Christ. It is not out of antiquarian allegiance that we love the truths of Scripture—even the hard ones. It is out of love to Christ—and love to the people that only the Christ of truth can save.

---

2. Dorothy Sayers, *A Matter of Eternity*, ed. Rosamond Kent Sprague (Grand Rapids, MI: Eerdmans, 1973), 86.

Heavenly Father, we tremble and groan
at the revelation of everlasting torment.
Oh, how great is the sin of man! Our sin.
Help us not to measure the justice of hell
by our meager sense of sin,
but rather to get a just sense of our sin
by the measure of the horror of hell.
May we fear it rightly.
May we rescue as many as we can.
May we cherish the Christ who bore our guilt.
May we stand in awe of Your justice and grace.
In Jesus' name we pray. Amen.

thirteen

TO YOU WHO BELIEVE, HE IS PRECIOUS

A Meditation on 1 Peter 2:7

"TO YOU...WHO BELIEVE, [CHRIST] IS PRECIOUS" (1 Peter 2:7, RSV). The mark of a child of God is not perfection, but hunger for Christ. If we have tasted the kindness of the Lord, we will desire him (1 Peter 2:2–3). The reason for this is that a child has the nature of its father. We are partakers of the divine nature (2 Peter 1:4) if we are born of God and have His seed abiding in us (1 John 3:9). We are, as it were, chips off the Old Block. For 1 Peter 2:4 says Christ is precious to God, and 1 Peter 2:7 says therefore He is precious to believers. Therefore belief which saves is not just agreeing that the Bible is true. Belief which saves signifies a new nature that cherishes what God cherishes.

In light of this, consider John 17:26. What a promise this is! Here Jesus is praying for His disciples and all who would believe on Him through their word (John 17:20). He concludes His prayer with the highest petition of all: "I made known to them your name, and I will make it known, that the love with which you have loved me may be in them, and I in them."

Look carefully. Jesus' request to God is that God's love for the Son be in us. Have you ever thought that Jesus wants you to love Him not merely with your love but with the love which God the Father has for Him? How is this possible? It is possible because of the new birth. Becoming a Christian means getting a new nature, which is given by God. Practically speaking this means that God comes into our lives by the Holy Spirit and begins to give us new affections, new emotions, namely the emotions of God. It is the presence of God the Spirit in our lives that causes us to love Jesus with the love of God the Father. Indeed the Holy Spirit may be viewed as the love of God in a Person. To be ruled by the Spirit is to be ruled by a divine love for Jesus. Jesus is simply praying that we may be filled with the Spirit who is the divine Person who expresses the love that the Father has for the Son. Thus we will be filled with the very love with which the Father loves the Son.

And what a love that is! There is no greater love in all the universe than the love flowing between the Father and the Son in the holy Trinity. No love is more powerful, more intense, more continuous, more pure, more full of delight in the beloved, than the love God the Father has for the Son. It is an energy of joy that makes atom bombs look like firecrackers. Oh, how the Father delights in the Son! Oh, how precious the Son is to the Father! "This is my beloved Son, with whom I am well pleased," God said at Jesus' baptism (Matthew 3:17). "This is my beloved Son, with whom I am well pleased; listen to him," God said at the transfiguration (Matthew 17:5).

In all the universe none is more precious to God the Father than His Son, Jesus Christ. That is how precious He should be to us. And with what infinite energy does the Father love the Son! That is the greatness to which we are moving in our delight in the Son. O Christian, join the Father in this greatest of all loves! If you are born of God, see Jesus with the eyes of God. "To you who believe, He is precious."

Father, please answer Your Son's prayer
for us even now as much as we can bear—
that the love with which You loved
Him may be in us and He in us.
We confess that our love for
Christ is not all He deserves.
We long to love Him more.
More purely. More intensely.
More consistently. More joyfully.
For Your own sake, Father,
and for the glory of Your Son,
satisfy us with His glory.
In His name we pray. Amen.

fourteen

WHAT DOES
JESUS WANT?

What does Jesus want? We can see the answer in His prayers. What does He ask God for? His longest prayer is John 17. Here is the climax of His desire:

> Father, I desire that they also, whom you have given me, may be with me where I am (verse 24).

Among all the undeserving sinners in the world, there are those whom God has "given to Jesus." These are those whom God has drawn to the Son (John 6:44, 65). These are *Christians*—people who have "received" Jesus as the crucified and risen Savior, Lord, and Treasure of their lives (John 1:12; 3:17; 6:35; 10:11, 17–18; 20:28). Jesus says He wants them to be with Him.

Sometimes we hear people say that God created man because He was lonely. So they say, "God created us so that we would be *with Him*." Does Jesus agree with this? Well, He *does* say that He really wants us to be with Him! Yes, but why? Consider the rest of the verse. Why does Jesus want us to be with Him?

> [Father, I desire that they may be with me] *to see my glory* that you have given me because you loved me before the foundation of the world.

That would be a strange way of expressing His loneliness. "I want them with me so they can see my glory." In fact, it doesn't express His loneliness. It expresses His concern for the satisfaction of *our* longing, not His loneliness. Jesus is not lonely. He and the Father and the Spirit are profoundly satisfied in the fellowship of the Trinity. We, not He, are starving for something. And what Jesus wants is for us to experience what we were really made for—seeing and savoring His glory.

Oh, that God would make this sink into our souls! Jesus made us (John 1:3) to see His glory. Just before He goes to the cross He pleads His deepest desires with the Father: "Father, I *desire*—I desire!—that they…may be with me where I am, *to see my glory.*"

But that is only half of what Jesus wants in these final, climactic verses of His prayer. I just said we were really made for seeing *and savoring* His glory. Is that what He wants—that we not only see His glory but savor it, relish it, delight in it, treasure it, love it? Consider verse 26, the very last verse:

> I made known to them your name, and I will continue to make it known, *that the love with which you have loved me may be in them*, and I in them.

That is the end of the prayer. What is Jesus' *final* goal for us? Not that we simply see His glory, but that we love Him with the same love that the Father has for Him: "that the love with

which you [Father] have loved me may be in them." Jesus' longing and goal is that we see His glory and then that we be able to
love what we see with the same love that the Father has for the
Son. And He doesn't mean that we merely *imitate* the love of the
Father for the Son. He means the Father's very love becomes our
love for the Son—that we love the Son with the love of the
Father for the Son. This is what the Spirit becomes and bestows
in our lives: Love for the Son by the Father through the Spirit.

What Jesus wants most is that His elect be gathered in
(John 10:16; 11:52) and then get what *they* want most—to *see*
His glory and then *savor* it with the very savoring of the Father
for the Son.

What I want most is to join you (and many others) in seeing
Christ in all His fullness, and that we together be able to love what
we see with a love far beyond our own half-hearted human capacities.

This is what Jesus prays for us: "Father, show them my
glory and give them the very delight in me that you have in me."
Oh, may we *see* Christ with the eyes of God and *savor* Christ
with the heart of God. That is the essence of heaven. That is the
gift Christ came to purchase for sinners at the cost of His death
in our place.

Holy Father, we join Jesus in praying for
ourselves what He prayed for us.
Grant us to be with Him that we might see
His glory and love Him with the
very love You have for Him.
Let us, we pray, have as much of that
experience of Christ now as we can.
Then complete it in heaven with Him
by the power that raised Him from the dead.
We want to see Him.
We want to savor His glory.
O merciful father, open our eyes and lead us home.
In Jesus' name we pray. Amen.

fifteen

HOW DOES THE LAW HELP ME KNOW MY SIN?

A Meditation on Romans 7:7–8

What then shall we say? That the law is sin? By no means!
Yet if it had not been for the law, I would not have known sin.
I would not have known what it is to covet if the law had not said,
"You shall not covet." But sin, seizing an opportunity through the
commandment, produced in me all kinds of covetousness.
Apart from the law, sin lies dead.

LET'S BEGIN BY LOOKING AT THE CONTEXT OF ROMANS 7:7–8.

1. Paul is defending the law after saying some pretty negative things about it (like: You need to die to the law, 7:4; sinful passions are aroused by the law, 7:6; the law came in so that transgressions would increase, 5:20).

2. His defense is that the law is not sin, but exposes sin as sin and, in doing so, often makes sin flare up and then gets blamed for it.

3. There is a sinful condition beneath our sins that we need to know about. Paul says in verse 8, "Sin…produced in me all kinds of covetousness." In other words, the sin of coveting is

produced by a condition called "sin." This is our "depravity," or "fallenness," or (for Christians) our "remaining corruption."

4. Paul uses the commandment against covetousness to illustrate how the law shows us our sinful condition.

5. "Covetousness" simply means desires that you shouldn't have. At root what makes bad desires bad is that they come as a loss of satisfaction in all that God is for us in Jesus. Desires are bad that come from a loss of contentment in God.

6. Until God's law comes in and prohibits some of our desires ("You shall not covet"), our desires are not experienced as sin but as imperial demands that seem to have their own lawful standing. Until God's law confronts this mutinous "law" we don't experience our desires as sin ("apart from the law sin lies dead," 7:8). "I want it, so I should have it." This is inborn. "Desire equals deserve," until God's law says, no. You see this clearly in little children for whom it is very painful to learn that their desires are not law.

7. This points to the root sinful condition: independence from God, rebellion against God. At root our sinful condition is the commitment to be our own god. I will be the final authority in my life. I will decide what is right and wrong for me; and what is good and bad for me; and what is true and false for me. My desires express my sovereignty, my autonomy, and—though we don't usually say it—my presumed deity.

This independence from God—this rebellion and presumed sovereignty and autonomy and deity—produces *all kinds* of covetousness. This word "all (kinds)" sets us to thinking about how deviously covetousness can express itself. We need to know this or we won't know our sin or ourselves.

In general, there are two kinds of bad desire (covetousness) that the law stirs up, and both are expressions of our love affair with independence and self-exaltation.

1. One is more obvious, namely, desires for the very things that are forbidden. Proverbs 9:17 says, "Stolen water is sweet, and bread eaten in secret is pleasant." St. Augustine confessed that as a youth, "I was willing to steal, and steal I did, although I was not compelled by any lack, unless it were the lack of a sense of justice or a distaste for what was right and a greedy love of doing wrong.... *I had no wish to enjoy the things I coveted by stealing, but only to enjoy the theft itself and the sin.*"[1] So one form of desire that the commandment stirs up is the desire to do the very thing forbidden. This is owing to our ingrained love of being our own god and our distaste for submission.

2. The other kind of bad desire that the law stirs up is the desire to keep the law by our own strength with a view to exalting our own moral prowess. This looks very *different*. No stealing, no murder, no adultery, no lying. Instead, just self-righteousness. Not that keeping the law is evil or covetous. No, the problem is the desire to keep it by *my* power, not in childlike reliance on *God's* power. The problem is desiring the glory of my achievement, not God's. That is a subtle form of covetousness.

---

1. Augustine, *Confessions,* II, 4, emphasis added.

So know yourself! Know your sins. Know your sinful condition of rebellion and insubordination. If this leads you (again
and again) to the cross and the gospel of justification by grace
alone through faith alone, it will exalt Christ, be healing to your
soul, and sweetening to all your relationships.

Father, thank You for the painful
work of the law in our lives.
Thank You that You did not leave us
feeling fine in our rebellion, but made us miserable.
Thank You for making us dejected in
the worship of our own divinity.
Oh, how precious is Your convicting law!
It awakens even now both trembling and treasuring.
Keep using it to show us Christ.
Enable us, as justified sinners, to delight in
Your law by Your redeeming power.
In Jesus' name we pray. Amen.

sixteen

A PASSION FOR PURITY
VERSUS PASSIVE PRAYER

I say to you that everyone who looks at a woman with lustful
intent has already committed adultery with her in his heart.
If your right eye causes you to sin, tear it out and throw it away.
For it is better that you lose one of your members
than that your whole body be thrown into hell.
MATTHEW 5:28–29

WHEN YOU ARE ENTICED SEXUALLY, DO YOU FIGHT WITH your mind to say no to the image and then mightily labor to fill your mind with counter-images that kill off the seductive image? "If by the Spirit you put to death the deeds of the body, you will live" (Romans 8:13).

Too many people think they have struggled with temptation when they have prayed for deliverance and hoped the desire would go away. That is too passive. Yes, God works in us to will and to do His good pleasure! But the effect is that we "work out [our] own salvation with fear and trembling" (Philippians 2:12–13). Gouging out your eye may be a metaphor, but it means something very violent. The brain is a "muscle" to be flexed for purity, and in the Christian it is supercharged with the Spirit of Christ.

What this means is that we must not give a sexual image or impulse more than five seconds before we mount a violent counterattack with the mind. I mean that! Five seconds. In the first two seconds we shout, "NO! Get out of my head!" In the next two seconds we cry out: "O God, in the name of Jesus, help me. Save me now. I am Yours."

Good beginning. But then the real battle begins. This is a mind war. The absolute necessity is to get the image and the impulse out of our mind. How? Get a Christ-exalting, soul-captivating counter-image into the mind. Fight. Push. Strike. Don't ease up. It must be an image that is so powerful that the other image cannot survive. There are lust-destroying images and thoughts.

For example, have you ever in the first five seconds of temptation demanded of your mind that it look steadfastly at the crucified form of Jesus Christ? Picture this. You have just seen a peek-a-boo blouse inviting further fantasy. You have five seconds. "No! Get out of my mind! God help me!" Now, immediately, demand of your mind—you can do this by the Spirit (Romans 8:13)—demand of your mind that it fix its gaze on Christ on the cross. Use all your fantasizing power to see His lacerated back. Thirty-nine lashes left little flesh intact. He heaves with His breath up and down against the rough vertical beam of the cross. Each breath puts splinters into the lacerations. The Lord gasps. From time to time He screams out with intolerable pain. He tries to pull away from the wood and the massive spokes through His wrists rip into the nerve endings and He screams again with agony and pushes up with His feet to give some relief to His wrists. But the bones and nerves in His pierced feet crush against each other with anguish and He screams again. There is no relief. His throat is raw from screaming and thirst. He loses His breath and thinks He is suffocating, and suddenly His body involuntarily gasps for air and all the injuries unite in pain. In torment, He forgets about the crown of two-inch thorns and throws His head back in desperation, only to hit one of the thorns perpendicular against the cross beam and drive it half an inch into His skull. His voice reaches a soprano pitch of pain and sobs break over His pain-wracked body as every cry brings more and more pain.

Now, I am not thinking about the blouse anymore. I am at Calvary. These two images are not compatible. If you will use the muscle of your brain to pursue—violently pursue with the muscle of your mind—images of Christ crucified with the same creative energy that you use to pursue sexual fantasies, you will kill them. But it must start in the first five seconds—and not give up.

So my question is: Do you fight, rather than only praying and waiting and trying to avoid? It is image against image. It is ruthless, vicious mental warfare, not just prayer and waiting. Join me in this bloody warfare to keep my mind and body pure for my Lord and my wife and my church. Jesus suffered beyond imagination to "purify for himself a people for his own possession" (Titus 2:14). Every scream and spasm was to kill my lust—"He himself bore our sins in his body on the tree, that we might die to sin and live to righteousness" (1 Peter 2:24).

Father, have mercy on us in our continual battle with lust.

Oh, how we love the victories You give.

Let us live there more and more.

Grant us the will to say no to every temptation.

Yes, Lord, grant us far more than to say no.

Help us fight.

Give us the will to make war on our impurities.

Show us the infinite and all-satisfying

glory of the crucified Christ.

May Your name be so precious to us

that we absolutely will not defile it.

In Jesus' mighty name we pray. Amen.

THE BATTLE FOR
BREAKFAST BLESSING

A Meditation on Ephesians 4:29–5:2

THIS IS FOR FAMILIES. THE REST OF YOU WILL, I HOPE, be helped also. I am assuming that Christian families try to eat breakfast together—or have some kind of family moment in the Word and prayer before going their different ways. Even if there are seasons in life when this is hard or impossible, not to work toward it seems contrary to Deuteronomy 6:7, "You shall teach [God's Word] diligently to your sons and shall talk of them…*when you rise up*" (NASB).

This takes effort. Everybody likes to get up at different times. So you have to decide how important you think these family moments in the Word are. It is possible—for little ones and teenagers and parents. You may have to work at it. But it can be done.

But once you are there, then what? For many of us, morning is our moodiest, least cheerful time of day. Teenagers, some say, are not fully human till midmorning. Dad may feel tremendous pressure looming ahead. Mom may be exhausted from a hundred pressures. Little ones may be cranky.

What then is the point of this family event? Dad, the point is for you to dispense grace to your family. If there's no dad, then, mom, it's your job. How do you dispense grace?

Here's a key part of the answer from Ephesians 4:29:

> Let no unwholesome word proceed from *your mouth*, but only such a word as is good for edification according to the need of the moment, *so that it will give grace to those who hear.* (NASB)

The key dispenser of grace is the dad's mouth. O Fathers! What a treasure is the grace that comes from your mouth at the breakfast table!

1. Speak no unwholesome word.
No spoiled word. No unhelpful word. What does this mean? Well, perhaps the best interpretation is simply the next phrase where it is put positively:

2. Speak only words that are good for edification.
Aim always to build the faith of your family by what you say. Don't confuse this with building their egos. We are not talking here about self-esteem. We are talking about building faith and hope in Jesus Christ. "Edification" means growing confidence in the promises of God purchased by the blood of Christ. Dads, come to breakfast with some word of hope for your family. Tell them something about God and Christ that will help them be strong that day.

3. Speak words that fit the need of the moment.

Some promises are more fitting than others. If they are old enough, ask your children what their needs and challenges will be for that day. Or ask them the night before. Give them something from God that will help them be strong in the strength in the Lord that day.

4. This is the way you dispense grace to your family.

But it assumes something. Namely, that anger is not the dominant feeling in your heart. Some anger is godly. Most is not. So Paul continues, "Let all bitterness and wrath and anger and clamor and slander be put away from you, along with all malice" (Ephesians 4:31, NASB). Malicious anger is deadly. One of its most deadly effects is to ruin a dad's ability to bless his family with his mouth. His heart is so angry that his mouth is continually sour. Oh, for sweetness in the mouth of a dad! Oh, for deeply delighting dads! "I will bless the LORD at all times; his praise shall continually be in my mouth" (Psalm 34:1). That is what blessing the family assumes.

How can you get there, dads? Answer:

[Forgive, just] as God in Christ forgave you. Therefore be imitators of God, as beloved children. And walk in love, as Christ loved us and gave himself up for us. (Ephesians 4:32–5:2)

Dads, do you know the sweetness of being forgiven a million-dollar debt? Have you seen Jesus suffering horrifically to purchase your forgiveness? Do you know the wonder of hearing God call to you, "Beloved child"? Not just child. But *loved* child.

So, dads, get up early enough to soak in these things for your own soul. Then you will bring the aroma of Christ to the table. In the long run, no matter how grumpy the family may seem, this blessing will come back on your head a thousandfold.

Gracious Father, please give us the will
to work for family togetherness in Your Word.
Forgive us for all the past failures.
Don't let us be paralyzed.
Push us to plan and don't let us coast.
Give to us fathers, especially, a humble,
overflowing, hope-filled gratitude for Your grace.
Let it spill on our families every day.
In Jesus' name. Amen.

eighteen

YOU HAVE ONE PRECIOUS LIFE

Is TV Too Big a Part of It?

IF ALL OTHER VARIABLES ARE EQUAL, YOUR CAPACITY TO know God deeply will probably diminish in direct proportion to how much television you watch. There are several reasons for this. One is that television reflects American culture at its most trivial. And a steady diet of triviality shrinks the soul. You get used to it. It starts to seem normal. Silly becomes funny. And funny becomes pleasing. And pleasing becomes soul-satisfaction. And in the end the soul that is made for God has shrunk to fit snugly around triteness.

This may be unnoticed, because if all you've known is American culture, you can't tell there is anything wrong. If you have only read comic books, it won't be strange that there are no novels in your house. If you live where there are no seasons, you won't miss the colors of fall. If you watch fifty TV ads each night, you may forget there is such a thing as wisdom. TV is mostly trivial. It seldom inspires great thoughts or great feelings with glimpses of great Truth. God is the great, absolute, all-shaping Reality. If He gets any air time, He is treated as an opinion. There is no reverence. No trembling. God and all that He thinks about the world is missing. Cut loose from God, everything goes down.

Just think how new TV is. In the 2000 years since Christ, TV has shaped only the last 2.5 percent of that history. For 97.5 percent of the time since Jesus, there was no TV. And for 95 percent of this time there was no radio. It arrived on the scene in the early 1900s. So for 1900 years of Christian history, people spent their leisure time doing other things. We wonder, what could they possibly have done? They may have read more. Or discussed things more. For certain they were not bombarded with soul-shrinking, round-the-clock trivialities.

Do you ever ask, "What could I accomplish that is truly worthwhile if I did not watch TV?" You see, it isn't just what TV does to us with its rivers of emptiness; it is also what TV keeps us from doing. Why not try something? Make a list of what you might accomplish if you took the time you spend watching TV and devoted it to something else. For example:

- You might be inspired to some great venture by learning about the life of a noble saint like Amy Carmichael and how she found courage to go alone to serve the children of India. Where do such radical dreams come from? Not from watching TV. Open your soul to be blown away by some unspeakable life of dedication to a great cause.

- You might be inspired by a biography of a businessman or doctor or nurse to work hard for the skills to bless others with the excellence of your profession devoted to a higher end than anything you will see commended on TV, which never includes Jesus Christ.

- You might memorize the eighth chapter of Paul's letter to the Romans, and penetrate to the depths of his vision of God, and discover the precious power of memorized Scripture in your life and ministry to others. No one could estimate the power that would come to a church if we all turned the TV off for one month and devoted that same amount of time to memorizing Scripture.

- You might write a simple poem or a letter to a parent or a child or a friend or a colleague expressing deep gratitude for their life or a longing for their soul.

- You might make a cake or a casserole for new neighbors and take it to them with a smile and an invitation to visit some time and get to know each other.

So there are good reasons to try a TV fast. Or to simply wean yourself off of it entirely. We have not owned a TV for thirty-four years of marriage except for three years in Germany when we used it for language learning. There is no inherent virtue in this. I only mention it to prove that you can raise five culturally sensitive and Biblically informed children without it. They never complained about it. In fact they often wondered out loud how people found the time to watch as much as they do.

Heavenly Father, help us know the
wonders of Your Word and your world.
Keep us from the trivializing effects of our culture.
Help us fight for the joy of seeing great things.
Put us out of taste with trifles.
Grant the weight of glory—
Your glory—to rest upon us.
So make us a humble, wise, loving
people for Your great name's sake.
In Jesus' name. Amen.

nineteen

TERRORISM, JUSTICE, AND LOVING OUR ENEMIES

September 11, 2001

SOMEONE ASKED ME AFTER OUR TUESDAY PRAYER SERVICE in response to the terrorist attacks on September 11, 2001, "Can we pray for justice, and yet love our enemy at the same time?" The answer is yes.

But let's start with our own guilt. Christians know that if God dealt with us only according to justice, we would perish under His condemnation. We are guilty of treason against God in our sinful pride and rebellion. We deserve only judgment. Justice alone would condemn us to everlasting torment.

But God does not deal with us only in terms of justice. Without compromising His justice He "justifies the ungodly" (Romans 4:5). That sounds unjust. And it *would* be if it were not for what God did in the life and death of Jesus Christ. The mercy of God moved Him to send the Son of God to bear the wrath of God so as to vindicate the justice of God when He justifies sinners who have faith in Jesus. So we have our very life because of mercy *and* justice (Romans 3:25–26). They met in the cross.

So we are not quick to demand justice unmingled with mercy. Jesus demands, "Love your enemies and pray for those who persecute you, so that you may be sons of your Father who is in heaven. For he makes his sun rise on the evil and on the good, and sends rain on the just and the unjust" (Matthew 5:44–45). And, of course Jesus modeled this for us as a perfect man. "*While we were enemies* we were reconciled to God by the death of his Son" (Romans 5:10). And even as He died for His enemies He prayed, "*Father, forgive them*, for they know not what they do" (Luke 23:34).

So the resounding command of the apostles is, "Bless those who persecute you; bless and do not curse…. Repay no one evil for evil…. Never avenge yourselves, but leave it to the wrath of God, for it is written, 'Vengeance is mine, I will repay, says the Lord.' To the contrary, 'if your enemy is hungry, feed him; if he is thirsty, give him something to drink'" (Romans 12:14–20). When we live this way, we magnify the glory of God's mercy and the all-satisfying Treasure that He is to our souls. We show that because of His supreme value to us, we do not need the feeling of personal vengeance in order to be content.

But it does not compromise this truth to say that God should also be glorified as the one who governs the world and delegates some of His authority to civil states. Therefore some of God's divine rights as God are given to governments for the purposes of restraining evil and maintaining social order under just laws. This is what Paul means when he writes, "There is no authority except from God, and those that exist have been instituted by God.... [This authority is] God's servant for your good...he does not bear the sword in vain. For he is the servant of God, an avenger who carries out God's wrath on the wrong-doer" (Romans 13:1–4).

God wills that human justice hold sway among governments, and between citizens and civil authority. He does not prescribe that governments always turn the other cheek. The government "does not bear the sword in vain." Police have the God-given right to use force to restrain evil and bring law-breakers to justice. And legitimate states have the God-given right to restrain life-threatening aggression and bring criminals to justice. If these truths are known, this God-ordained exercise of divine prerogative would glorify the justice of God who mercifully ordains that the flood of sin and misery be restrained in the earth.

Therefore, we will magnify the *mercy* of God by praying for our enemies to be saved and reconciled to God. At the personal level we will be willing to suffer for their everlasting good and we will give them food and drink. We will put away malicious hatred and private vengeance. But at the public level we will also magnify the *justice* of God by praying and working for justice to be done on the earth, if necessary through wise and measured force from God-ordained authority.

Heavenly Father, forgive us for our impure anger
and our defiled sense of justice.
We know our righteous indignation is
mingled with unholy fear and selfishness.
Purge our motives from all sin.
Make our courage clean and our pursuit of justice pure.
Cause us to abound in love to our enemies.
Forbid that we would fail to feel the
way You have loved us even while we resisted Your will.
Oh, that the world of Islam would see the difference between
Western culture and true Christianity.
Let them see the truth that Christians suffer for their enemies.
In Jesus' name. Amen.

twenty

HOW IS GOD'S LOVE EXPERIENCED IN THE HEART?

EXPERIENCING THE LOVE OF GOD, NOT JUST THINKING about it, is something we should desire with all our hearts. This is an experience of great joy because in it we taste the very reality of God and His love. It is the ground of deep and wonderful assurance—the assurance that our hope "does not disappoint" (Romans 5:5, NASB). This assurance helps us "rejoice in hope of the glory of God" (Romans 5:2). It carries us through terrible trials of faith.

Is this experience of the love of God the same for all believers? No, not in degree. If all believers had the same experience of the love of God, Paul would not pray for the Ephesians that they "have strength to comprehend with all the saints what is the breadth and length and height and depth, and to know the love of Christ that surpasses knowledge" (Ephesians 3:18–19). He prayed this, because some (or all!) were deficient in their experience of this love of God in Christ. And presumably we are not all deficient in exactly the same way.

How then do we pursue the fullness of the experience of the love of God poured out in our hearts by the Holy Spirit? One key is to realize that the experience is not like a hypnosis or electric shock or drug-induced hallucinations or shivers at a good tune. Rather it is mediated through knowledge. It is not the same as knowledge. But it comes through knowledge. Or to say it another way, this experience of the love of God is the work of the Spirit giving unspeakable joy in response to the mind's perception of the demonstration of that love in Jesus Christ. In this way, Christ gets the glory for the joy that we have. It is a joy in what we see in Him.

Where can you see this in the Scriptures? Consider 1 Peter 1, "Though you have not seen him, you love him. Though you do not now see him, you believe in him and rejoice with joy that is inexpressible and filled with glory" (verse 8). Here is an experience of great and inexpressible joy. Joy beyond words. It is not based on a physical seeing of Christ. But it is based on believing in Christ. Christ is the focus and content of the mind in this inexpressible joy.

In fact, 1 Peter 1:6 says that the joy itself is "in" the truth that Peter is telling us about the work of Christ. It says, "In *this* you rejoice." And what is "this"? It is the truth that 1) in "His great mercy, [God] has caused us to be born again to a living hope through the resurrection of Jesus Christ from the dead" (verse 3); and 2) we will obtain "an inheritance that is imperishable, undefiled, and unfading" (verse 4); and 3) we "are being guarded through faith for a salvation ready to be revealed in the last time" (verse 5). In *this* we greatly "rejoice with joy that is inexpressible and filled with glory" (verse 8). We know something. In *this* we rejoice! The experience of unspeakable joy is a mediated experience. It comes through knowledge of Christ and His work. It has content.

Consider also Galatians 3:5, "Does he who supplies the Spirit to you and works miracles among you do so by the works of the law, or by hearing with faith?" We know from Romans 5:5 that the experience of the love of God is "through the Holy Spirit who has been given to us." But now Galatians 3:5 tells us that this supply of the Spirit is not without content. It is "by *hearing* with *faith*." Two things: hearing and faith. There is the hearing of the truth about Christ, and there is the faith in that truth. This is how the Spirit is supplied. He comes *through knowing and believing*. His work is a mediated work. It has mental content. Beware of seeking the Spirit by emptying your head.

Similarly Romans 15:13 says that the God of hope fills us with joy and peace "*in believing*." And believing has content. The love of God is experienced in knowing and believing Christ because, as Romans 8:39 says, the love of God is "in Christ Jesus our Lord." Nothing will be able to separate us from the love of God, which *is in Christ Jesus* our Lord.

So do four things: look, pray, renounce, enjoy.

1. Look to Jesus. Consider Christ. Meditate on His glory and His work, not just casually, but intentionally. Think about the promises He made and guaranteed by His death and resurrection.
2. Pray that God would open your eyes to the wonder of His love in these things.

3. Renounce all known attitudes and behaviors that contradict this demonstration of love to you.
4. Then enjoy the experience of the love of God poured out in your heart by the Holy Spirit.

Father, incline our hearts to see the
beauty of Christ and to embrace it with joy.
Grant that we would behold and believe—
that we would see and savor.
May our minds lay hold on the content of faith,
and our hearts receive it with the affection of faith.
Cause Your love to flow like a river through our souls.
May we not just know about it,
but experience the reality of it, to the glory of Christ.
In His name. Amen.

twenty-one

REASONS BELIEVERS IN CHRIST NEED NOT BE AFRAID

OVER A HUNDRED TIMES IN THE BIBLE WE ARE TOLD not to be afraid. "Fear not, for I am with you; be not dismayed, for I am your God" (Isaiah 41:10). When we are young we are easily made afraid, though our knowledge of what can harm us is small. As we get older, our knowledge of risk and peril increases. Must our fears increase? One might answer no, because we also become wiser and more able to avoid danger and avert peril and overcome assault.

But there are better reasons not to let our fears increase. It is not so much because we become smarter or more able to avoid danger, but that we become more confident that, by faith in Jesus, God will take care of us in the way He sees best. It does not guarantee safety or comfort in this life. But it does guarantee everlasting joy, as we trust in Him. Trusting God, through Jesus Christ, is the key to fearlessness. And promises from God are the key that leads from the dungeon of fear. So consider these and be courageous.

1. We will not die apart from God's gracious decree for His children.

> If the Lord wills, we will live and do this or that. (James 4:15)

> "Are not two sparrows sold for a penny? And not one of them will fall to the ground apart from your Father. But even the hairs of your head are all numbered. Fear not, therefore; you are of more value than many sparrows." (Matthew 10:29–31)

> See now that I, even I, am he, and there is no god beside me; I kill and I make alive; I wound and I heal; and there is none that can deliver out of my hand. (Deuteronomy 32:39) (See also Job 1:21; 1 Samuel 2:6; 2 Kings 5:7.)

2. Curses and divination do not hold sway against God's people.

> For there is no enchantment against Jacob, no divination against Israel. (Numbers 23:23)

3. The plans of terrorists and hostile nations do not succeed apart from our gracious God.

> The LORD brings the counsel of the nations to nothing; he frustrates the plans of the peoples. (Psalm 33:10)

> Take counsel together [you peoples], but it will come to nothing; speak a word, but it will not stand, for God is with us. (Isaiah 8:10) (See also 2 Samuel 7:14; Nehemiah 4:15.)

4. Man cannot harm us beyond God's gracious will for us.

> The LORD is on my side; I will not fear. What can man do to me? (Psalm 118:6)

> In God I trust; I shall not be afraid. What can man do to me? (Psalm 56:11)

5. God promises to protect His own from all that is not finally good for them.

> Because he holds fast to me in love, I will deliver him; I will protect him, because he knows my name. (Psalm 91:14)

6. God promises to give us all we need to obey, enjoy, and honor Him forever.

> Therefore do not be anxious, saying, "What shall we eat?" or "What shall we drink?" or "What shall we wear?"...Your heavenly Father knows that you need them all. But seek first the kingdom of God and his righteousness, and all these things will be added to you. (Matthew 6:31–33)

> And my God will supply every need of yours according to his riches in glory in Christ Jesus. (Philippians 4:19)

7. God is never taken off guard.

> Behold, he who keeps Israel will neither slumber nor sleep. (Psalm 121:4)

8. God will be with us, help us, and uphold us in trouble.

> "Fear not, for I am with you; be not dismayed, for I am your God; I will strengthen you, I will help you, I will uphold you with my righteous right hand." (Isaiah 41:10)

> "For I, the LORD your God, hold your right hand; it is I who say to you, 'Fear not, I am the one who helps you.'" (Isaiah 41:13)

9. Terrors will come, some of us will die, but not a hair of our heads will perish.

> Then [Jesus] said to them, ". . . there will be terrors and great signs from heaven.... and some of you they will put to death.... But not a hair of your head will perish." (Luke 21:10–11, 18)

10. Nothing befalls God's own but in its appointed hour.

> So they were seeking to arrest him, but no one laid a hand on him, because his hour had not yet come. (John 7:30) (See also John 8:20; 10:18.)

11. When God Almighty is your helper, none can harm you beyond what He decrees.

> So we can confidently say, "The Lord is my helper; I will not fear; what can man do to me?" (Hebrews 13:6)

> If God is for us, who can be against us? (Romans 8:31)

12. *God's faithfulness is based on the firm value of His name, not the fickle measure of their obedience.*

> And Samuel said to the people, "Do not be afraid; you have done all this evil…. For the LORD will not forsake his people, for his great name's sake." (1 Samuel 12:20–22)

13. *The Lord, our protector, is great and awesome.*

> Do not be afraid of them. Remember the Lord, who is great and awesome. (Nehemiah 4:14)

Great God of promise, grant us to believe what You have said.
Take away our doubting. Don't let us be like Peter,
halfway across the waves of obedience, sinking for fear.
Fix our minds and hearts firmly on Your
Word and make us lionhearted in our love for others.
Oh, that Your church would be the happiest, boldest,
most unwavering risk-takers in the cause of justice and love!
In Jesus' all-providing name we pray. Amen.

EMBRACING THE PAIN OF SHAME

A Meditation on Acts 5:41

THERE IS A KIND OF SHAME THAT YOU SHOULD NOT BE ashamed of. You might say, "Well, then it is not really shame." But the Bible calls it shame, and it really feels like shame—until the miracle happens in our heart that turns our felt values upside down.

The reason this is important to me is that I am still learning—sometimes I think, just beginning to learn—how to embrace this shame. I mean really embrace, not just tolerate, the unpleasant feeling of being shamed. Until I learn this more fully, I will never be the kind of witness among unbelievers that God calls me to be.

Where do I get this strange notion of embracing shame? I get it from the story of Peter and the apostles in Acts 5. They were arrested and put in jail for healing and for preaching Christ (verse 18). That night the angel of the Lord released them and told them to go preach in the temple "all the words of this Life" (verse 20). But again the Council and the High Priest took them into custody and accused them of "filling Jerusalem with [their] teaching" (verse 28). "We strictly charged you not to teach in this name."

Peter spoke up with boldness and said, "We must obey God rather than men" (verse 29). The Council was ready to kill them when Gamaliel, a teacher of the law, stood up and said, "If this plan or this undertaking is of men, it will fail; but if it is of God, you will not be able to overthrow them. You might even be found opposing God" (verses 38–39). At this they changed their plans and "beat them and charged them not to speak in the name of Jesus, and let them go" (verse 40).

Now comes one of the most stunning verses in the New Testament: "So they went on their way from the presence of the Council, rejoicing that they had been considered worthy to suffer shame for His name" (verse 41, NASB). Read that slowly and let it sink in. Notice two things.

First, they were shamed. They "suffered shame." To be made a spectacle by the respected leaders of your people and to be treated like wicked criminals and to be stripped to the waist (at least) and to be hurt so badly that you probably scream out and cry with deep sobs of pain—that is a shame-filled moment. The Bible calls it shame. It feels like shame. And it is horrible.

Second, they rejoiced over this shame. Use your imagination. This is not light. It is not romantic. It is not a noble, heroic moment with soaring music and lots of admirers watching. This is terrifying. The pain is excruciating. Death may follow. There is no recourse. It is humiliating. But the apostles did not sue.

They did not seethe at the loss of their rights. They did not swear at their enemies. Instead they sang. They rejoiced "that they had been considered worthy to suffer shame for His name."

That is what I mean by "embracing the pain of shame." Are you there yet? If not, take heart. Not many of us are. Do you want to be? So do I. What shall we do? Three things:

1. Let's pray for each other. Be specific. Pray, *Father, work a deep transforming work in us so that we actually feel joy when we are shamed for the name of Christ.*
2. Meditate often on the infinite worth of Christ, the sweetness of His promises, and the great suffering that He endured for your salvation.
3. Take a step into uncharted territory to witness to Christ. If the painful feelings of shame come, transpose that dirge into a song of triumph.

Then the world will begin to see what is really most valuable in the universe, Jesus Christ. Until then, we look so much like them in what we enjoy, they see little reason to pay any attention.

O Father, forgive us for fearing to be shamed
for the name of Your Son.
Grant us the mantle of Peter who rejoiced over shame.
Incline us to meditate day and night
on the sufferings of Christ.
Oh, that we would see and feel what
He was willing to suffer to make us
courageous in the cause of love.
May the gospel of Christ run and triumph
through our joyful readiness to be shamed
for the name of Jesus.
In that name we pray. Amen.

twenty-three

HOW JESUS HELPED HIS DISCIPLES INCREASE THEIR FAITH

A Meditation on Luke 17:5–10

⁵ The apostles said to the Lord, "Increase our faith!" ⁶ And the Lord said, "If you had faith like a grain of mustard seed, you could say to this mulberry tree, 'Be uprooted and planted in the sea,' and it would obey you. ⁷ Will any one of you who has a servant plowing or keeping sheep say to him when he has come in from the field, 'Come at once and sit down at table'? ⁸ Will he not rather say to him, 'Prepare supper for me, and dress properly, and serve me while I eat and drink, and afterward you will eat and drink'? ⁹ Does he thank the servant because he did what was commanded? ¹⁰ So you also, when you have done all that you were commanded, say, 'We are unworthy servants; we have only done what was our duty.'"

IN LUKE 17:5 THE APOSTLES ASK JESUS TO INCREASE their faith. How does Jesus help them? In two ways, both of which are by telling them truth. So even in the *way* He responds

He shows us that faith comes by hearing. Knowing certain things should increase our faith.

First, He strengthens our faith by telling us in verse 6 that the crucial issue in accomplishing great things to advance the kingdom of God is not the *quantity* of our faith, but the power of God. He says, "If you had faith like a grain of mustard seed, you could say to this mulberry tree, 'Be uprooted and be planted in the sea,' and it would obey you." By referring to the tiny mustard seed after being asked about increased faith, He deflects attention away from the quantity of faith to the object of faith. *God* moves mulberry trees. And it does not depend decisively on the quantity of our faith, but on His power and wisdom and love. In knowing this, we are helped not to worry about our faith and are inspired to trust God's free initiative and power.

Second, He helps our faith grow by telling us in verses 7–10 that when we have done all we are commanded to do, we are still radically dependent on grace. Jesus gives an illustration. You might want to read it again in verses 7–10. The gist of it is that the owner of a slave does not become a debtor to the slave no matter how much work the slave does. The meaning is that God is never our debtor. Verse 10 sums it up: "So you also, when you have done all that you were commanded, say, 'We are unworthy servants; we have only done what was our duty.'" We are always His debtor. And we will never be able to pay this debt, nor are we ever meant to. We will always be dependent on grace. We will never work our way up out of debt to a place where God is in *our* debt. "Who has given a gift to [God] that he might be repaid?" (Romans 11:35).

When it says in verse 9 that the owner does not "thank" the slave, the idiom for "thank" is provocative. I think the idea is that "thanks" is a response to grace. The reason the owner does not thank the slave is that the servant is not giving the owner more than what the owner deserves. He is not treating the owner with *grace*. Grace is being treated better than you deserve. That's how it is with us in relation to God. We can *never* treat God with grace. We can never give Him more than He deserves. Which means that He never owes us thanks. God never says "Thank you" to us. Instead He is always giving us more than what we deserve, and *we* are always owing *Him* thanks.

So the lesson for us is that when we have done all we should do—when we have solved all our church problems, and fixed the attitudes of all Christian people, and mobilized many missions, and loved the poor, and saved marriages, and reared godly children, and kept every promise we've made, and fulfilled all business responsibilities, and boldly proclaimed Christ— God owes us no thanks. Instead we will at that moment relate to Him as debtors to grace just as we do now.

This is a great encouragement to faith. Why? Because it means that God is just as free to bless us *before* we get our act together as He is *after*. Since we are "unworthy" slaves before we have done what we should, and "unworthy" slaves afterwards as well, it is only grace that would prompt God to help us. Therefore He is free to help us before and after. This is a great incentive to trust Him for help when we feel like our act is not together. And this trust is exactly what obtains the power to get our act together.

So two things increase our faith.

1. God Himself, and not the quantity of our faith, is the decisive factor in flinging mulberry trees out of the way.
2. Free grace is decisive in how God treats us before and after we have done all we ought to do.

We never move beyond the need for grace. Therefore let us trust God for great things in our little faith, and let us not be paralyzed by what is left to be done in our personal lives, and in our church, and in our vocations, and in the global cause of missions.

Father of mercy, and God of all grace,
what a wonder You are!
We love to ponder the truth that You
never thank us for anything, and that this is sweet.
You are never in our debt. We are ever in Yours.
We owe You everything. And You love to have it that way.
You, getting the praise and the thanks;
we, getting the help and the joy.
There is where we want to stay.
Oh, to be at home in the welfare
of Your everlasting bounty!
We thank You, in Jesus' name. Amen.

twenty-four

THE STRANGE WAYS
OF OUR
WONDERFUL BUILDER

WAS CHRIST BUILDING HIS CHURCH ON SEPTEMBER 11, 2001 when the World Trade Center towers came down? Or when your own world collapsed? The reason this question rises is the absolute, universal authority behind Jesus' promise in Matthew 16:18, "I will build my church." Who said this? The one who spoke and fevers departed (Luke 4:39), trees withered (Mark 11:21), demons obeyed (Mark 1:27), Satan was plundered (Mark 3:27), wind ceased (Mark 4:41), the dead were raised (Luke 7:14; John 11:43), thousands ate from five loaves and two fish (Matthew 14:19–21), and water became wine (John 4:46) or a walkway for His feet (Matthew 14:25).

This power over heaven and earth and hell is explicitly related to Christ's missionary commitment to build His church. "I will build my church, and the gates of hell shall not prevail against it" (Matthew 16:18). "All authority in heaven and on earth has been given to me. Go therefore and make disciples of all nations" (Matthew 28:18–19). In other words, Jesus is firmly committed to use His power over heaven and earth and hell to make disciples. No event in the universe which Christ produces or permits is outside His purpose to build His church.

But it doesn't look that way. His ways are not our ways. He seldom moves in a straight line from A to B. The way up is almost always down. The river turns back on itself flowing away from the sea even as it moves toward the sea. I tried to catch this once in a poem about Hosea's pain-filled life:

> Think not, my son, that God's great river
>> Of love flows simply to the sea,
> He aims not straight, but to deliver
>> The wayward soul like you and me.
> Follow the current where it goes,
>> With love and grace it ever flows.

The surprising, convoluted path of God in redemptive history brings Paul to these words, "Oh, the depth of the riches and wisdom and knowledge of God! How unsearchable are his judgments and how inscrutable his ways!" (Romans 11:33).

For example, was Christ triumphantly building His church when He was killed by His enemies and buried for three days? Jesus answers: "Destroy this temple, and in three days I will raise it up" (John 2:19). "I lay down my life for the sheep. And I have other sheep that are not of this fold…. No one takes it from me…I have authority to lay it down, and I have authority to take it up again" (John 10:15–16, 18). In other words, what looked like failure and tragedy was total authority—plus the purchase of "other sheep." By the worst sin that has ever been committed—the murder of the Son of God—Jesus was triumphantly building His church.

Was Christ building His church when the apostle Paul was imprisoned in Rome? Paul answers: "What has happened to me has really served to advance the gospel, so that it has become known throughout the whole imperial guard and to all the rest that my imprisonment is for Christ. And most of the brothers, having become confident in the Lord by my imprisonment, are much more bold to speak the word without fear" (Philippians 1:12–14). I am "bound with chains as a criminal. But the word of God is not bound!" (2 Timothy 2:9). In other words, what looked like defeat was Christ's strange design for victory.

Was Christ building His church in China when the Communists triumphed in 1949, ending 150 years of Protestant missionary presence?

> The growth of the Church in China since 1977 has no parallels in history.... Mao Zedong unwittingly became the greatest evangelist in history.... [He] sought to destroy all religious 'superstition' but in the process cleared spiritual roadblocks for the advancement of Christianity. Deng [Xiaoping] reversed the horrors inflicted by Mao and in freeing up the economy, gave more freedom to the Christians.... [Today] the Church of the Lord Jesus is larger than the Communist Party of China.[1]

---

1. Patrick Johnstone and Jason Mandryk, *Operation World: When We Pray God Works,* 21st Century Edition (Waynesboro, GA: Paternoster, 2001), 161. The second sentence is from the 1993 edition of *Operation World,* 164.

So then, was this all-ruling Christ building His church on September 11? I answer with questions that are not merely hypothetical. What if Christ saw the planes heading for the destruction of thousands and the upheaval of nations? What if, at the same time, He saw 200 million Hindu untouchables in India, the Dalits? What if He saw that His centuries-long work of dislodging them from Hindu bondage was about to come to consummation in our day and they were contemplating embracing Islam or possibly Christianity or Buddhism? And what if He foresaw that this Islam-related terror against civilians in New York would have a mass effect of tilting millions of Dalits away from Islam toward Christ? What if He withheld His power from stopping the terrorists because (along with ten thousand other hope-filled effects) He had a view to the ever-lasting life of millions of untouchables in India? And if not this, perhaps my grandchildren will tell a better story of sovereign grace, which only time reveals.

*Almighty God and Father, steady our hands
on the plow of obedience when we face terrible sufferings.
Remind us and assure us that You
are sovereign and You are good.
Forbid that we would ever murmur against
You in Your inscrutable wisdom.
Make us confident that all authority is
Yours and that You are building Your church
invincibly, even when apparent defeat abounds.
In the mighty name of Jesus. Amen.*

twenty-five

A·N·T·H·E·M
STRATEGIES FOR
FIGHTING LUST

I HAVE IN MIND MEN AND WOMEN. FOR MEN IT'S OBVIOUS. The need for warfare against the bombardment of visual temptation to fixate on sexual images is urgent. For women it is less obvious, but just as great if we broaden the scope of temptation to food or figure or relational fantasies. When I say "lust" I mean mainly the realm of thought, imagination, and desire that envisions what God forbids and often leads to sexual misconduct.

I don't mean sex is bad. God created it. He blessed it. He made it pleasurable. And He defined the place for it, to protect the beauty and power of it, namely, marriage between a man and a woman. But it has become disordered with the fall of man into sin. Therefore, we must exercise restraint and make war on what would destroy us. Here is one set of strategies in the war against wrong desires. I put it in the form of an acronym,
A•N•T•H•E•M.

A—AVOID as much as is possible and reasonable the sights and situations that arouse unfitting desire. I say "possible and reasonable" because some exposure to temptation is inevitable. And I say "unfitting desire" because not all desires for sex, food, and family are bad. We know when they are unfitting and unhelpful and on their way to becoming enslaving. We know our weaknesses and what triggers them. "Avoiding" is a biblical strategy. "Flee youthful passions and pursue righteousness" (2 Timothy 2:22). "Make no provision for the flesh, to gratify its desires" (Romans 13:14).

N—Say NO to every lustful thought within five seconds.[1] And say it with the authority of Jesus Christ. "In the name of Jesus, NO!" You don't have much more than five seconds. Give it more unopposed time than that, and it will lodge itself with such force as to be almost immovable. Say it out loud if you dare. Be tough and warlike. As John Owen said, "Be killing sin or it will be killing you."[2] Strike fast and strike hard. "Resist the devil, and he will flee from you" (James 4:7).

T—TURN the mind forcefully toward Christ as a superior satisfaction. Saying no will not suffice. You must move from defense to offense. Fight fire with fire. Attack the promises of sin with the promises of Christ. The Bible calls lusts "*deceitful* desires" (Ephesians 4:22). They lie. They promise more than they can deliver. The Bible calls them "passions of your former *ignorance*" (1 Peter 1:14). Only fools yield. "All at once he fol-

---

1. For more on this, see chapter 16.
2. John Owen, *The Mortification of Sin,* in *The Works of John Owen,* ed. William H. Gould, vol. 6 (London: Johnstone & Hunter, 1852; reprint, Edinburgh and Carlisle, Penn.: Banner of Truth, 1959), 9.

lows her, as an ox goes to the slaughter" (Proverbs 7:22). Deceit is defeated by truth. Ignorance is defeated by knowledge. It must be glorious truth and beautiful knowledge. This is why I wrote *Seeing and Savoring Jesus Christ* (Crossway, 2001). I need short portraits of Christ to keep myself awake spiritually to the superior greatness of Jesus. We must stock our minds with the promises and pleasures of Jesus. Then we must turn to them immediately after saying, "NO!"

H—HOLD the promise and the pleasure of Christ firmly in your mind until it pushes the other images out. "Fix your eyes on Jesus" (Hebrews 3:1). Here is where many fail. They give in too soon. They say, "I tried to push the fantasy out, and it didn't work." I ask, "How long did you try?" How hard did you exert your mind? Remember, the mind is a muscle. You can flex it with vehemence. Take the kingdom violently (Matt. 11:12). Be brutal. Hold the promise of Christ before your eyes. Hold it. Hold it! Don't let it go! Keep holding it! How long? As long as it takes. Fight! For Christ's sake, fight till you win! If an electric garage door were about to crush your child you would hold it up with all your might and holler for help, and hold it and hold it and hold it and hold it. More is at stake, Jesus said, in the habit of lust (Matthew 5:29).

E—ENJOY a superior satisfaction. Cultivate the capacities for pleasure in Christ. One reason lust reigns in so many is that Christ has so little appeal. We default to deceit because we have little delight in Christ. Don't say, "That spiritual talk is just not me." What steps have you taken to waken affection for Jesus? Have you fought for joy? Don't be fatalistic. You were created to treasure Christ with all your heart—more than you treasure sex or chocolate or sugar. If you have little taste for Jesus, competing pleasures will triumph. Plead with God for the satisfaction you don't have: "Satisfy us in the morning with your steadfast love, that we may rejoice and be glad all our days" (Psalm 90:14). Then look, look, look at the most magnificent Person in the universe until you see Him the way He is.

M—MOVE into a useful activity away from idleness and other vulnerable behaviors. Lust grows fast in the garden of leisure. Find a good work to do, and do it with all your might. "Do not be slothful in zeal, be fervent in spirit, serve the Lord" (Romans 12:11). "Be steadfast, immovable, always abounding in the work of the Lord" (1 Corinthians 15:58). Abound in work. Get up and do something. Sweep a room. Hammer a nail. Write a letter. Fix a faucet. And do it for Jesus' sake. You were made to manage and create. Christ died to make you "zealous for good deeds" (Titus 2:14). Displace deceitful lusts with a passion for good deeds.

Merciful Father, how often have we failed to fight lust!
We have embraced the enemy that makes war on our souls.
Forgive us according to Your promise to be
slow to anger and abounding in mercy.
Come now and give us new resolve,
and new power, and a new view of Your
promises and Your supreme value.
Satisfy us in the evening with Your steadfast love,
and sever the root of lust with a superior pleasure.
In Jesus' pure and powerful name. Amen.

twenty-six

MEALTIME PRAYERS WITH THE PIPERS

I WROTE THE FOLLOWING MEALTIME PRAYERS FOR MY own family to use. There is a short one and a longer one for each of the three meals in the day. The three longer ones have been used by our family for over twenty years, and all the children know the prayers by heart now so that they are able to say them together without reading.

For example, in August of 2001, when Benjamin, my second oldest son, was married in Brazil, I was asked to say a table grace at a large family gathering in Fortaleza. Instead of praying by myself, I said, "I think what I would like to do is ask all my children (Karsten, Benjamin, Abraham, Barnabas, Talitha) to pray with Noël and me the evening prayer that we have used during all their growing up years." Then we all prayed the prayer from memory. The people were so moved that the whole family could say the prayer together in unison on the spur of the moment that they asked me to pray it again slowly and have it translated into Portuguese one phrase at a time. It proved to be a wonderful witness for Christ to all the people there.

So I offer them here, not with the expectation that everyone will use them, but with the hope they will stir up serious reflection on what we really want God to do at mealtimes and what we are truly thankful for.

MORNING MEAL
(SHORT)
Lord Jesus, thank You for this day,
And for the night of rest,
And for this food, and for the way
That we are always blessed.

MORNING MEAL
(LONGER)
Our Father, every day You give
The food by which our bodies live.
For this we thank You from our heart
And pray that as we this day start,
You might allow our eyes to see
Your endless generosity.
And grant that when we thus are filled,
We may do only what You've willed.

MIDDAY MEAL
(SHORT)
Lord Jesus, Thank You for these gifts
And what each one displays;
For Your own steady love which lifts
Our hearts in midday praise.

MIDDAY MEAL
(LONGER)

We're grateful, Father, for this hour
To rest and draw upon Your power
Which You have shown in sun and rain
And measured out to every grain.
Let all this food which You have made
And graciously before us laid
Restore our strength for these next hours
That You may have our fullest power.

EVENING MEAL
(SHORT)

Lord Jesus, come now to our meal,
And bless to us this food;
Where faith is weak, dear Lord, reveal
That all You give is good.

EVENING MEAL
(LONGER)

How faithful, Father, is Your care;
Again as always food is there.
Again You have set us before
A meal we pray will mean much more
Than single persons filled with food;
Let there be, Lord, a loving mood.
And as You make our bodies new,
Come now and feed our oneness too.

Gracious Father, You are a prayer-hearing God.
We want to commune with You in prayer all day long.
We thank You for every gift we have—
life, breath, and everything.
Teach us how to weave spontaneous expressions of
exultation (and desperation) together with disciplined,
regular times of prayer—like mealtimes.
Never let us drift from the sweet habits of gratitude.
Call us to prayer again and again.
Hear us in Jesus' name. Amen.

twenty-seven

IT IS NEVER RIGHT TO BE ANGRY WITH GOD

RECENTLY I SAID THOSE WORDS TO A GROUP OF SEVERAL hundred people: "It is never, ever, ever, right to be angry with God." There was an incredulous look on many faces. This was not landing well. Clearly many did not agree.

Some were obviously tracking with me, but others looked baffled. I have given a lot of thought to those baffled looks since then. What assumptions were out there that made this statement so difficult to accept? To me nothing could be more obvious. Why is it then so confusing to some others?

There are two possible assumptions that may be common in many heads today, which would make people balk at what I said.

First, many assume that feelings are not right or wrong, they are neutral. So to say that anger (whether at God or anybody else) is "not right" is like saying sneezing is not right. You don't apply the labels right and wrong to sneezing. It just happens to you. That is the way many people think about feelings: they just happen to you. Therefore, they are not moral or immoral; they are neutral. So for me to say that it is never right to be angry with God is to put the feeling of anger in a category where it doesn't belong, the category of morality.

This kind of thinking about feelings is one of the reasons there is so much shallow Christianity. We think the only things that have moral significance in the world are acts of reflection and volition. And we think feelings like desire and delight and frustration and anger are not acts of volition, but waves that break on the shore of our souls with no moral significance. Small wonder that many people do not earnestly seek to be transformed at the level of feelings, but only of "choices." That makes for a superficial saint (at best).

This assumption is contrary to what the Bible teaches. In the Bible, many feelings are treated as morally good and many as morally bad. What makes them good or bad is how they relate to God. If they show that God is true and valuable, they are good, and if they suggest that God is false or foolish or evil, they are bad. For example, delight in the Lord is not neutral, it is commanded (Psalm 37:4). Therefore it is good. But to "take pleasure in wickedness" is wrong (2 Thessalonians 2:12), because it signifies that sin is more desirable than God, which is not true.

It's the same with anger. Anger at sin is good (Mark 3:5), but anger at goodness is sin. That is why it is never right to be angry with God. He is always and only good, no matter how strange and painful His ways with us. Anger toward God signifies that He is bad or weak or cruel or foolish. None of those is true, and all of them dishonor Him. Therefore it is never right to be angry at God. When Jonah and Job were angry with God, Jonah was rebuked by God (Jonah 4:9) and Job repented in dust and ashes (Job 42:6).

The second assumption that may cause people to stumble over the statement that it is never right to be angry with God is the assumption that God really does things that ought to make us angry at Him. But, as painful as His providence can be, we should trust that He is good, not get angry with Him. That would be like getting angry at the surgeon who cuts us. It might be right if the surgeon slips and makes a mistake. But God never slips.

I have learned over the years that when a person uses the words, "Is it right to be angry at God?" he may be asking a very different question. He may be asking, "Is it right to *express* anger at God?" These are not the same question, and the answer is not always the same.

The question usually arises in times of great suffering and loss. Disease threatens to undo all your dreams. Death takes a precious child from your family. Utterly unexpected desertion and divorce shake the foundations of your world. At these times people can become very angry at God.

Is this right? To answer this question we might, perhaps, ask the angry person, Is it *always* right to get angry at God? In other words, can a person get angry at God for every reason, and still be right? Was it right, for example, for Jonah to be angry at God's mercy on Nineveh? "God relented of the disaster that he had said he would do to them, and he did not do it. But it displeased Jonah exceedingly, and he was *angry*" (Jonah 3:10–4:1). I assume the answer would be no. We should not get angry at God for just any reason.

But then we would ask: Which deeds of God should make us angry with Him, and which should not? Now this is harder to answer. The truth begins to close in on the angry heart.

What about the things that displease us? Are these the acts of God that justify our anger at Him? Is it the acts of God that hurt us? "I kill and I make alive; I wound and I heal; and there is none that can deliver out of my hand" (Deuteronomy 32:39). Are these the acts that justify us in directing our anger at God? Or is it His choice to permit the devil to harass and torture us? "The LORD said to Satan, 'Behold, [Job] is in your hand; only spare his life.' So Satan went out from the presence of the LORD and struck Job with loathsome sores from the sole of his foot to the crown of his head" (Job 2:6–7). Does the decision of God to permit Satan to hurt us and our children justify our anger *at Him*?

Or come at it from the other side. What is anger? The common definition is: "An intense emotional state induced by displeasure" (Merriam-Webster). But there is an ambiguity in this definition. You can be "displeased" by a *thing* or by a *person*. Anger at a thing does not contain indignation at a choice or an act. We simply don't like the effect of the thing: the broken clutch, or the grain of sand that just blew in our eye, or rain on our picnic. But when we get angry at a person, we are displeased with a choice they made and an act they performed. Anger at a person always implies strong disapproval. If you are angry at me, you think I have done something I should not have done.

This is why being angry at God is never right. It is wrong—always wrong—to disapprove of God for what He does and permits. "Shall not the Judge of all the earth do what is just?" (Genesis 18:25). It is arrogant for finite, sinful creatures to disapprove of God for what He does and permits. We may weep over the pain. We may be angry at sin and Satan. But God is always righteous in what He does and what He permits. "Yes, O Lord God, the Almighty, true and righteous are Your judgments" (Revelation 16:7).

But many who say that it is right to *be* angry with God really mean it is right to *express* anger at God. When they hear me say it is wrong to *be* angry with God, they think I mean "stuff your feelings and be a hypocrite." That's not what I mean. I mean it is always wrong to disapprove of God in any of His judgments.

But if we do experience the sinful emotion of anger at God, what then? Shall we add the sin of hypocrisy to the sin of anger? No. If we feel it, we should confess it to God. He knows it anyway. He sees our hearts. If anger at God is in our heart, we may as well tell Him so, and then tell Him we are sorry, and ask Him to help us put it away by faith in His goodness and wisdom.

When Jesus died on the cross for our sins, He removed forever the wrath of God from all who trust Him. God's disposition to us now is entirely mercy, even when severe and disciplinary (Romans 8:1). Therefore, doubly shall those in Christ turn away from the terrible specter of anger at God. We may cry, in agony, "My God, My God, where are you?" But we will follow soon with, "Into your hands I commit my spirit."

So I say it again: It is never right to be angry with God. But if you sin in this way, don't compound it by hypocrisy. Tell Him the truth and repent.

Heavenly Father, please forgive us for the
times we have indicted You with our anger.
Oh, how fragile is our faith in Your
perfect goodness and power and wisdom.
Strengthen our confidence that You are
never worthy of our anger or accusation.
Make us humble.
May we put our hands on our mouths
in tragedy and feel the truth:
The Judge of all the earth will do right.
In Jesus' name. Amen.

twenty-eight

THE CHURCH WAS SPOKEN AGAINST EVERYWHERE

CAN THE GOSPEL SPREAD, AND THOUSANDS BE converted, and churches grow, and love abound where Christianity is continually spoken against? Yes. It not only can; it has. I say this not to discourage winsomeness, but to encourage hope. Do not assume that seasons of hostility or controversy will be lean seasons with little power or growth. They may be seasons of explosive growth and great spiritual blessing.

How do we know this? Consider the way Luke reports the state of the church in the book of Acts. When Paul finally gets to Rome near the end of his life, he invites the "local leaders of the Jews" to come hear his gospel. What these leaders say about the "sect" of Christians is very significant. They say, "With regard to this sect we know that it is spoken against everywhere" (Acts 28:22).

This is not surprising to disciples who knew that Jesus said, "You will be hated by all nations for my name's sake" (Matthew 24:9). And: "Woe to you, when all men speak well of you" (Luke 6:26). And: "If they have called the master of the house

Beelzebul, how much more will they malign those of his household!" (Matthew 10:25).

The early church was an embattled church. Yes, there were seasons of calm (Acts 9:31); but that was the exception. Most of the time there were slanders and misunderstandings and accusations and persecutions, not to mention internal disputes about ethics and doctrine. Virtually all of Paul's letters reflect controversy in the church as well as affliction from outside. The point is not that this is desirable, but that it need not hinder great power and growth. In fact, it may be the occasion and reason for great power and growth.

This seems to be Luke's view, because, even though he portrayed Christianity as "spoken against everywhere," he also portrayed relentless growth throughout the book of Acts. "The Lord added to their number day by day those who were being saved" (Acts 2:47). "The disciples were increasing in number" (Acts 6:1). "The word of God continued to increase, and the number of the disciples multiplied greatly" (Acts 6:7). "The hand of the Lord was with them, and a great number who believed turned to the Lord" (Acts 11:21). "The word of God increased and multiplied" (Acts 12:24). "The churches...increased in number daily" (Acts 16:5). "All the residents of Asia heard the word of the Lord" (Acts 19:10). "The word of the Lord continued to increase and prevail mightily" (Acts 19:20).

Therefore, we must not think that controversy and conflict keep the church from experiencing the power of the Holy Spirit and dramatic growth. We are taught in Romans 12:18, "If possible, so far as it depends on you, live peaceably with all." But we are not taught to sacrifice truth for peace. So Paul said, "Even if we or an angel from heaven should preach to you a gospel contrary to the one we preached to you, let him be accursed" (Galatians 1:8).

And if there is enough conflict and hostility that those who speak the gospel are even imprisoned, that very moment of bad press may be the occasion of gospel triumph. Why? Because, Paul said, "I am suffering, bound with chains as a criminal [for the gospel]. But the word of God is not bound!" (2 Timothy 2:9). In fact, it may be that when God and truth are loved enough that we are willing to take stands that incur slander and hostility, the Spirit may move more powerfully than in times of peace and popularity.

Sometimes Christians have favor with society and sometimes we "are spoken against everywhere." In either case, God can, and often does, pour out His power for effective witness. Both peace and slander can be the occasion of blessing. Therefore let us not embrace the assumption that times of social ridicule must be times of weakness and fruitlessness for Christianity. They may be a sign of faithfulness and occasions of great harvest. The church was "spoken against everywhere," and "the word of the Lord continued to increase and prevail mightily."

*Father in Heaven, look upon the threats
against Your people and grant to Your servants to
continue to speak Your Word with all boldness.
Never let us grow weary in well-doing because of opposition.
Never let us despair that the Word of God is bound.
Keep us hoping and confident that You will build
Your church and glorify Your Son.
Use us in this great cause, we pray.
In Jesus' name. Amen.*

twenty-nine

BY WHAT DEATH WILL YOU GLORIFY GOD?

A Meditation on John 21:18–19

WHEN JOHN WROTE HIS GOSPEL, PETER HAD PROBABLY already been killed by the Roman emperor Nero. So when he recorded the words of Jesus about Peter's coming death, he was able to look back and interpret the symbolism Jesus had used. Here's what Jesus said to Peter, with John's interpretation:

> "Truly, truly, I say to you, when you were young, you used to dress yourself and walk wherever you wanted, but when you are old, you will stretch out your hands, and another will dress you and carry you where you do not want to go." (This he said to show by what kind of death he was to glorify God.) And after saying this he said to him, "Follow me." (John 21:18–19)

It is a sobering thing to be told by your Master and friend that you will die in His service. It was oblique, but Peter probably got the message. And who knows what look was on Jesus' face when He said it. But such is the price of following Jesus Christ. This isn't that different from what He predicts for each of us. "If anyone comes to me and does not hate…his own life, he cannot be my disciple" (Luke 14:26). "Whoever loves his life loses it, and whoever hates his life in this world will keep it for life eternal" (John 12:25). "If anyone would come after Me, let him deny himself and take up his cross and follow me" (Matthew 16:24). "Some of you will be put to death. You will be hated by all for my name's sake" (Luke 21:16–17).

Tradition says that Peter was crucified upside down in Rome during one of Nero's persecutions in the mid-sixties. The early church historian Eusebius wrote, "Peter seems to have preached in Pontus and Galatia and Bithynia and Cappadocia and Asia, to the Jews of the Dispersion, and at last, having come to Rome, he was crucified head downward, for so he himself had asked to suffer."[1]

Jesus predicted the martyrdom of Peter. Jesus knew what sort of death it would be and He knew the time frame. This much knowledge could discourage Peter. Or it could serve to remind him that, come what may, the Lord Jesus is never taken off guard. Not only that, Jesus spoke these words to Peter after rising triumphant from the dead. This meant that "Christ being raised from the dead will never die again; death no longer has dominion over him" (Romans 6:9). Therefore Jesus will be alive and ruling when Peter comes to die. He will be there to help him. "I am with you always, even to the end of the age" (Matthew 28:20). And not only to help him die, but raise him: "If the Spirit of Him who raised Jesus from the dead dwells in you, he who raised Christ Jesus from the dead will also give life to your mortal bodies" (Romans 8:11).

---

1. Eusebius, *Ecclesiastical History,* III, I.

Jesus knew that there would be part of Peter's will that would not want this death. "Another…will carry you where you do not want to go" (John 21:18). Even Jesus cried, "If it be possible, let this cup pass from me" (Matthew 26:39). So it is with all who follow in His steps. Pain is pain, not pleasure. Only a higher love brings you to embrace it when you could avoid it by denying Christ.

John said Peter's death was to glorify God, "This he said to show by what kind of death he was to *glorify God*" (John 21:19). The way John said this seems to show that he considers all our deaths as appointed for the glory of God. The difference is: With what kind of death will we glorify God?

Are you ready for this? Will you show God great in the way you die? Will you say, "To live is Christ, and to die is gain" (Philippians 1:21)? Will you call this ugly, defeated, torturing enemy sweet names? Will the loss of all your earthly family, friends, and possessions fade at the prospect of seeing and being with Christ?

After Jesus had predicted the horrible death of Peter, he said to him, "Follow me."

"Let us go to him outside the camp" (Hebrews 13:13).

Father, teach us to number our days
and to get a heart of wisdom.
Forbid that we join the world in forgetting
the certainty of our death.
Don't let us play with the preciousness of life.
Make us ready to die well by helping us live
well by helping us trust You well.
Don't let us be surprised by our suffering.
Don't let us be surprised by being cut off early from this life.
Don't let us balk at the betrayal of friends
and the blast of enmity.
Help us to embrace our lot and count it all joy,
and say, with Paul, "to live is Christ and to die is gain."
In Jesus' name. Amen.

thirty

JOHN G. PATON'S FATHER

A Key to His Courage

JOHN G. PATON WAS A MISSIONARY TO THE NEW Hebrides, today called Vanuatu, in the South Seas. He was born in Scotland in 1824. I write about him because of the courage he showed throughout his eighty-two years of life. I want to be courageous in the cause of Christ. I want you to be. And I especially want my children to be. So I ponder courage in others. Where does it come from? When I dig for the reasons that John Paton was so courageous, one reason I find is the deep love he had for his father.

The tribute Paton pays to his godly father is, by itself, worth the price of his *Autobiography*, which is still in print.[1] Maybe it's because I have four sons (and Talitha), but I wept as I read this section. It filled me with such longing to be a father like this.

---

1. James C. Paton, *John G. Paton : Missionary to the New Hebrides, An Autobiography Edited by His Brother* (Edinburgh: The Banner of Truth Trust, 1965, orig. 1889, 1891). I have tried to retell Paton's story in an audio CD available through Desiring God Ministries, entitled, "'You Will Be Eaten by Cannibals!' Courage in the Cause of World Missions: Lessons in the Life of John G. Paton."

There was a "closet" where his father would go for prayer as a rule after each meal. The eleven children knew it and they reverenced the spot and learned something profound about God. The impact on John Paton was immense.

> Though everything else in religion were by some unthinkable catastrophe to be swept out of memory, were blotted from my understanding, my soul would wander back to those early scenes, and shut itself up once again in that Sanctuary Closet, and, hearing still the echoes of those cries to God, would hurl back all doubt with the victorious appeal, "He walked with God, why may not I?"[2]

> How much my father's prayers at this time impressed me I can never explain, nor could any stranger understand. When, on his knees and all of us kneeling around him in Family Worship, he poured out his whole soul with tears for the conversion of the Heathen world to the service of Jesus, and for every personal and domestic need, we all felt as if in the presence of the living Savior, and learned to know and love him as our Divine friend.[3]

One scene best captures the depth of love between John and his father, and the power of the impact on John's life of uncompromising courage and purity. The time came in his early twenties for the young Paton to leave home and go to

2. James C. Paton, 8.
3. Ibid., 21.

Glasgow to attend divinity school and become a city missionary. From his hometown of Torthorwald to the train station at Kilmarnock was a forty-mile walk. Forty years later, Paton wrote:

> My dear father walked with me the first six miles of the way. His counsels and tears and heavenly conversation on that parting journey are fresh in my heart as if it had been but yesterday; and tears are on my cheeks as freely now as then, whenever memory steals me away to the scene. For the last half mile or so we walked on together in almost unbroken silence—my father, as was often his custom, carrying hat in hand, while his long flowing yellow hair (then yellow, but in later years white as snow) streamed like a girl's down his shoulders. His lips kept moving in silent prayers for me; and his tears fell fast when our eyes met each other in looks for which all speech was vain! We halted on reaching the appointed parting place; he grasped my hand firmly for a minute in silence, and then solemnly and affectionately said: "God bless you, my son! Your father's God prosper you, and keep you from all evil!"
>
> Unable to say more, his lips kept moving in silent prayer; in tears we embraced, and parted. I ran off as fast as I could; and, when about to turn a corner in the road where he would lose sight of me, I looked back and saw him still standing with head uncovered where I had left him—gazing after me. Waving my hat in adieu, I rounded the corner and out of sight in an

instant. But my heart was too full and sore to carry me further, so I darted into the side of the road and wept for a time. Then, rising up cautiously, I climbed the dike to see if he yet stood where I had left him; and just at that moment I caught a glimpse of him climbing the dike and looking out for me! He did not see me, and after he gazed eagerly in my direction for a while he got down, set his face toward home, and began to return—his head still uncovered, and his heart, I felt sure, still rising in prayers for me. I watched through blinding tears, till his form faded from my gaze; and then, hastening on my way, vowed deeply and oft, by the help of God, to live and act so as never to grieve or dishonor such a father and mother as he had given me.[4]

The impact of his father's faith and prayer and love and discipline was immeasurable. Let every father read and be filled with longing and firm resolve to love like this.

---

4. Ibid., 25–6.

Oh, how we love to call You Father!
Even if we have been let down by our earthly fathers
(as all of us have in some measure),
You have never failed us.
You are perfect in mercy and justice,
severity and kindness, firmness and sweetness.
Grant us who are fathers to be this for our children.
Make us love You more than we love them.
Show them that our massive love for them
is rooted in an even greater love for You.
Make them courageous in the confidence that their
Father in heaven will be what we have been for them,
only ten thousand times more.
In Jesus' name. Amen.

HELPING PEOPLE HAVE THE ASSURANCE OF SALVATION

CHRISTIANS ARE CALLED TO HELP FIGHT FOR THEIR OWN assurance and to help others fight for theirs. God means for us to know we are saved and to enjoy that bold confidence in the face of opposition and threat. "These things I have written to you who believe in the name of the Son of God, so that you may know that you have eternal life" (1 John 5:13). What then shall we say to each other to help maintain the assurance of salvation? Here's what I would say.

1. Full assurance is God's will for us.

> And we desire each one of you to show the same earnestness to have the full assurance of hope until the end. (Hebrews 6:11)

2. Assurance is partially sustained by objective evidences for Christian truth.

> To [his apostles] he presented himself alive after his suffering by many proofs, appearing to them during forty days. (Acts 1:3)

3. Assurance cannot neglect the painful work of self-examination.

> Examine yourselves, to see whether you are in the faith. Test yourselves. Or do you not realize this about yourselves, that Jesus Christ is in you?—unless indeed you fail the test! (2 Corinthians 13:5)

4. Assurance will diminish in the presence of concealed sin.

> When I kept silent about my sin, my body wasted away through my groaning all day long. (Psalm 32:3, NASB)

5. Assurance comes from hearing the Word of Christ.

> So faith comes from hearing, and hearing through the word of Christ. (Romans 10:17)

> These are written so that you may believe that Jesus is the Christ, the Son of God, and that believing you may have life in his name. (John 20:31)

6. Repeated focusing on the sufficiency of the cross of Christ is crucial for assurance.

> Since we have a great priest over the house of God, let us draw near with a true heart in full assurance of faith. (Hebrews 10:21–22)

7. We must pray for eyes to see the truths that sustain assurance.

> I pray that the eyes of your heart may be enlightened, so that you will know what is the hope of His calling, what are the riches of the glory of His inheritance in the saints, and what is the surpassing greatness of His power toward us who believe. (Ephesians 1:18–19, NASB)

8. Assurance is not easily maintained in personal isolation.

> And the eye cannot say to the hand, "I have no need of you." (1 Corinthians 12:21)

> Exhort one another every day, as long as it is called "today," that none of you may be hardened by the deceitfulness of sin. (Hebrews 3:13)

9. Assurance is not destroyed by God's displeasure and discipline.

> Rejoice not over me, O my enemy; when I fall, I shall rise; when I sit in darkness, the LORD will be a light for me. I will bear the indignation of the LORD because I have sinned against him, until he pleads my cause and

executes judgment for me. He will bring me out to the light; I shall look upon his vindication. (Micah 7:8–9)

10. We must often wait patiently for the return of assurance.

I waited patiently for the LORD; he inclined to me and heard my cry. He drew me up from the pit of destruction, out of the miry bog, and set my feet upon a rock, making my steps secure. He put a new song in my mouth, a song of praise to our God. Many will see and fear, and put their trust in the LORD. (Psalm 40:1–3)

11. Assurance is a fight to the day we die.

Fight the good fight of faith. Take hold of the eternal life. (1 Timothy 6:12)

I have fought the good fight, I have finished the race, I have kept the faith. (2 Timothy 4:7)

12. Assurance is finally a gift of the Spirit.

The Spirit himself bears witness with our spirit that we are children of God. (Romans 8:16)

Whoever believes in the Son of God has the testimony in himself…. And this is the testimony, that God gave us eternal life, and this life is in his Son. (1 John 5:10–11)

Father of patience and mercy,
thank You for the gift of salvation and assurance.
Thank You for not leaving us without the Spirit to help us.
Thank You for working in us what is pleasing in Your sight.
Thank You for the cross of Christ that
helps us know the extent of our forgiveness.
Oh, help us look ever to Christ for our hope and joy.
Confirm our calling and election with the
evidences of grace in our lives.
In Jesus' name we ask these things. Amen.

The publisher and author would love to hear your
comments about this book. *Please contact us at:*
www.multnomah.net/johnpiper

DESIRINGGOD.ORG

DESIRING GOD *Ministries*

D esiring God Ministries exists to spread a passion for the supremacy of God in all things for the joy of all peoples through Jesus Christ. We have hundreds of resources available for this purpose, most of which are books, sermons, and audio collections by John Piper. Visit our website and discover

- free access to over twenty years of printed sermons by John Piper
- new, free downloadable audio sermons posted weekly
- many free articles and reviews
- a comprehensive on-line store where you may purchase John Piper's books and audio collections as well as God-centered children's curricula published by DGM
- information about DGM's conferences and international offices.

Designed for individuals with no available discretionary funds, DGM has a *whatever-you-can-afford* policy. Contact us at the address or phone number below if you would like more information about this policy.

DESIRING GOD MINISTRIES	DESIRING GOD MINISTRIES UNITED KINGDOM
2601 East Franklin Avenue Minneapolis, Minnesota 55406-1103 Toll free in the USA: 1-888-346-4700 International calls: (612) 373-0651 Fax: (612) 338-4372 *mail@desiringGOD.org* *www.desiringGOD.org*	Unit 2B Spencer House 14-22 Spencer Road Londonderry Northern Ireland BT47 6AA United Kingdom Tel/fax: 011 (02871) 342 907 *info@desiringgod.org.uk* *www.desiringGOD.org.uk*

DON'T MISS THESE
TITLES *from* JOHN PIPER

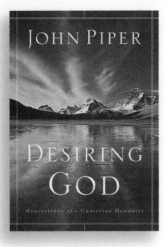

Desiring God

Delight is your duty. In this paradigm-shattering classic, newly revised and updated, John Piper reveals why the conflict between duty and pleasure doesn't truly exist.

ISBN 1-59052-119-6

The Dangerous Duty of Delight

Strengthen your relationship with God by simply enjoying Him! Discover just how to delight in the Lord in this compact version of John Piper's bestselling classic, *Desiring God*.

ISBN 1-57673-883-3

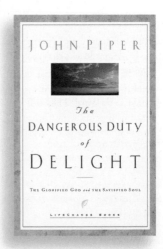

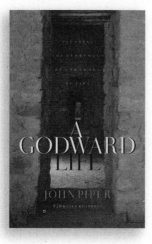

A Godward Life

Make God the center of your life and discover the radical difference by reading these 120 passionate thought-provoking devotions.

ISBN 1-57673-839-6

A Godward Life: Book Two

This follow-up to the popular *A Godward Life* is made up of 120 daily meditations that are solid meat and sweet milk from God's Word. They will brace your mind with truth and nourish your heart with God's sovereign grace.

ISBN 1-57673-405-6

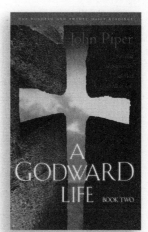

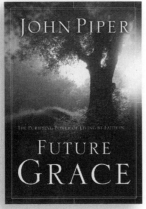

Future Grace

This book shows how the power of superior promises will sever the root of deceptive sin. It exposes the lie of Judas-joys.

ISBN 1-59052-191-9

The Pleasures of God

"God is most glorified in us when we are most satisfied in Him." This new edition of a classic by John Piper will further explore a life-changing essential—and again put God at the center, leaving the reader satisfied in Him.

ISBN 1-57673-665-2

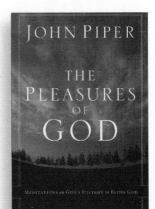